QUEENS
OF THE MERSEY

A SPECIAL HOMECOMING
TONY STOREY

Trinity Mirror Media

QUEENS
OF THE MERSEY

Trinity Mirror Media

QUEENS
OF THE MERSEY

A SPECIAL HOMECOMING

Editor: Tony Storey
Production: Harri Aston, Colin Harrison
Photography: Cunard, Mirrorpix, Cruise Media Services, PA Images, Mills Media,
Ron Jones (Merseyside Picture Library), Creative Photography, Newall Dunn Collection,
Deborah Lowndes, James Morgan and Robert Lloyd

Published by Trinity Mirror Media
Managing Director: Steve Hanrahan
Commercial Director: Will Beedles
Executive Editor: Paul Dove
Executive Art Editor: Rick Cooke
Senior Marketing Executive: Claire Brown
Sales & Marketing Manager: Elizabeth Morgan

The author and publishers are grateful to the following individuals for their time and help in
providing material for this book: Commodore Christopher Rynd, Captain Christopher Wells,
Michael Gallagher, Gill Haynes, Angus Struthers (Cunard Line); Commodore Bernard Warner,
Commodore Ronald Warwick, Captain Paul Wright, John Duffy, Eric Flounders (Cunard Line —
Retired); Captain Ian McNaught (Trinity House); Angie Redhead, Bob Swift (Cruise Liverpool);
Captain Robbie Quinn and Ken Moss (Mersey Ferries); Deborah Lowndes, Robert Lloyd.

First Edition
Published in Great Britain in 2015.
Published and produced by: Trinity Mirror Media,
PO Box 48, Old Hall Street, Liverpool L69 3EB.

ISBN: 9781910335154
Printed and bound by Zhongtian

Trinity Mirror Media

This book is dedicated to Mike Storey (1951 – 2014).

Mike discovered the Cunard experience late in his life,
but enjoyed every moment he spent on board
Queen Mary 2, Queen Victoria and Queen Elizabeth.

CONTENTS

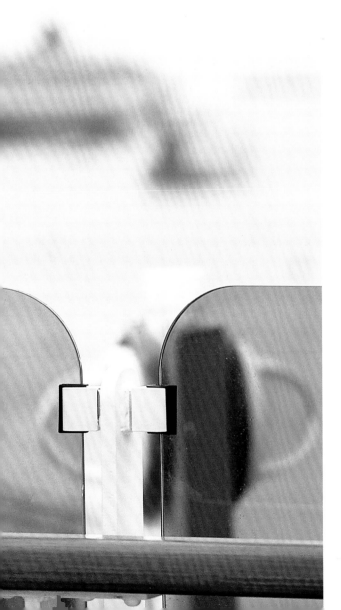

FOREWORD

The British and North American Royal Mail Steam Packet Company, universally (and thankfully!) called Cunard Line from the very beginning, was founded in Liverpool in May 1839 and for 128 years the headquarters of this proud shipping company was based in the city.

That means for 128 years the heartbeats of Cunard and Liverpool were together as one. Every Cunard ship had Liverpool emblazoned on their sterns and Liverpool was the hub of an enormous shipping empire.

When Britannia left Liverpool on that first crossing on 4 July, 1840, she changed the face of ocean travel forever which is why Cunard is proud to celebrate 175 years of uninterrupted service in 2015, and Liverpool should rejoice in 175 years of passenger shipping from the Mersey.

And celebrate we will on 25 May, 2015, when the current fleet – Queen Mary 2, Queen Victoria and Queen Elizabeth – gather together on the Mersey for the first time to salute Liverpool. The fleet, the three largest Cunarders ever built, have gathered together before but, given the backdrop and historic bond, this gathering will be the most magnificent of them all.

While it is true that Cunard's Head Office moved away in 1967 we have always been proud of coming from Liverpool and that pride is clearly evident. Over the last 25 years Cunard ships have made 21 visits to the Mersey and these visits have been history-making: from the one million who turned out to greet QE2 when she first called in 1990 to Queen Mary 2 becoming the largest passenger ship to sail up the Mersey in 2009. Each visit has drawn large crowds and will long be remembered by those drawn to the river to see a Cunarder coming home.

Tony Storey has done a great job recalling these visits and, as well as being delighted to be asked to write the foreword to what is a splendid book, I am very much looking forward to being onboard in command of Queen Victoria in May 2015 when the unique relationship Cunard and Liverpool share is celebrated.

Commodore Christopher Rynd
Cunard Line

LIVERPOOL
THE SPIRITUAL HOME OF CUNARD

Liverpool is the birthplace of Cunard, the city from which its first ship set sail and where many of its famous ocean liners were originally conceived

From the very beginning, the British and North American Royal Mail Steam Packet Company, universally called – also from the very beginning – Cunard Line, had its headquarters in Liverpool.

Although Samuel Cunard himself was based in Halifax, Nova Scotia, and latterly in London, one of his two senior partners, David McIver, to whom responsibility for day-to-day management of the company would fall, was already established as a ship manager in Liverpool.

The other senior partner, George Burns, whose chief task was to oversee construction, was based in Glasgow – and it was on the Clyde that the first 75 of the company's ships were built.

Cunard's first ship, Britannia, *pictured left*, departed on her maiden voyage from Liverpool to Boston via Halifax on 4 July, 1840.

The company originally opened offices in 1839 at 14 Water Street, and as the business prospered and expanded it moved – in August 1857 – to premises at 8 Water Street, on the corner with Rumford Street.

8 Water Street soon became the hub of an enormous empire, concerned not just with shipping across the Atlantic to the Unites States and Canada but also with routes to ports in the Mediterranean and the Middle East. By 1877 the company had 44 vessels – 19 on the Atlantic run, 12 in the Mediterranean and Black Sea services, and a further 13 serving Glasgow, Northern Ireland and Bermuda.

The first recorded visit by a senior royal to a Cunard ship took place in Liverpool on 11 July, 1913, when His Majesty King George V and Her Majesty Queen Mary visited the four-funnelled Mauretania.

Since then every reigning monarch has visited or travelled on Cunard ships, as have a great many other senior royals.

Following a further half-century of steady but consistent growth into one of the notable companies of the world, Cunard was ready to construct its own magnificent landmark building – a shoreside version of its floating palaces at sea.

It was clearly the headquarters of a company that mattered.

Cunard moved into its prestigious new building, its third and last in Liverpool, in June 1916 and it remained there for more than 50 years.

The Cunard Building was perfect in every way, not just for the reassurance it gave to passengers with its air of permanence, stability and grandeur, and not just from the efficiency of having the staff on one site, but because the directors could look out from the Boardroom window and see the divisions of their empire – the ships – coming and

Aquitania leaves Southampton after the war. She was eventually broken up after 36 years in service. Above right, Sir Samuel Cunard and opposite, the Cunard Building at Pier Head, Liverpool

going from the Mersey. But a significant change took place when, in 1919, Cunard moved its express liner passenger-mail service from Liverpool to Southampton.

Mauretania began the new Southampton to New York via Cherbourg service on 18 November 1919 and by the early 1920s Cunard's big three – Mauretania, Aquitania and Berengaria – were operating the weekly service from Southampton.

Since then Southampton has been the main UK departure point for the service to New York and the most famous ships ever built have been based in Southampton including the fabled Queens: Queen Mary and Queen Elizabeth. But while Cunard ships may have been based in Southampton all of them (until Queen Elizabeth 2 in 1969) had Liverpool on their sterns as their port-of-registry.

Cunard Building's walls could speak of many momentous decisions and the debates that led to them; there would have been the decision to build first the Queen Mary, and then Queen Elizabeth. Their detailed planning would have taken place within the Cunard Building as would the agonising decision to suspend construction of Queen Mary as the company's revenues collapsed in the Depression.

Here, Queen Elizabeth's secret, war-effort dash to the USA would have been planned, and other war services coordinated.

Another major event was the deliberations over the replacement for Queen Mary and Queen Elizabeth, and the eventual decision to build the truly revolutionary Queen Elizabeth 2. And after that decision was taken, following nerve-wracking false starts and near disasters, the Cunard Building became – along with the Clydeside shipyard itself – the powerhouse of design and decision-making that led to Cunard's most successful ship ever.

By 1967, the focus of Cunard activity had shifted away from Liverpool; it remained Cunard's administrative centre, but everything administered was elsewhere. The biggest supplier of company revenue was the USA and the home port for the Cunard fleet had been moving inexorably, and by now completely, to Southampton. And so, after 128 years in the city, Cunard's Head Office moved to New York in 1967 while its operational base moved to Southampton.

Sylvania's departure for New York on 30 November, 1967, would be the last sailing from Liverpool direct to New

Clockwise from above: Berengaria enters the River Tyne; Queen Elizabeth aground in Southampton waters in 1947; Cunard liner Sylvania, and Franconia tied up for an overhaul in Liverpool

York but the final passenger sailing from Liverpool would be made by Franconia on 30 January, 1968, to Bermuda and then New York. Interestingly, Cunard announced that sailings had been "suspended" from Liverpool and not formally stopped!

The fabled transatlantic service will "resume" from Liverpool on 4 July, 2015, when Queen Mary 2 departs for Halifax, Boston and New York – 175 years to the day since Britannia started the age of transatlantic passenger travel.

Following the departure of the Franconia from Liverpool in January 1968, all that remained of Cunard, housed in humbler quarters, was the cargo division. To all intents and purposes, Cunard had left home. However, the histories of Liverpool and Cunard are interwoven and the love of the company felt by the city remains evident each and every time a Cunard ship calls at the spiritual home.

Clockwise from top left: Finishing touches being made to QE2; Her Majesty launching the liner in 1967, the ship gathering speed as the stern enters the water, and crowds watching her make a splash following the ceremony at the John Brown yard in Clydebank

A view from the bridge of Queen Mary in 1934, during her construction. Right, on the River Clyde next to the paddle steamer Eagle III in 1936

1990

1994

1995

1999

1999

2000

2004

2007

2008

2010

2011

2011

2013

2013

2014

1996

2003

2009

2012

175 YEARS

CUNARD

THREE QUEENS, ONE MAGNIFICENT CITY

LIVERPOOL

24-26 MAY 2015

1990-2015

25 years of

CUNARD QUEENS

OF THE MERSEY

1990

QUEEN ELIZABETH 2, TUESDAY, 24 JULY

"Our passengers on the ferry? Well, for want of a
better word they were pretty dumbstruck!"

Captain Robbie Quinn, Mersey Ferry Royal Iris

Official estimates suggest a million people witnessed a moment in maritime history unfold along the River Mersey during a brilliant summer's day and evening on 24 July, 1990.

To mark the 150th anniversary of the start of Cunard's transatlantic service from the river in 1840, the then flagship of the British Merchant Fleet – Queen Elizabeth 2 – made her maiden call at the line's spiritual home.

Although Sir Samuel Cunard made Liverpool the global headquarters of his business in 1840, and the city retained that status until 1967, the spectacular call in 1990 marked the first time a Cunard Queen had sailed into the Mersey.

Her mighty "royal" predecessors on the Atlantic run, Queen Mary (launched on the Clyde in 1934) and Queen Elizabeth (launched four years later from the same John Brown yard) were too big to make it into the river, requiring a greater depth of water than was ever available at the Mersey Bar.

The fact that QE2 was going to mark that particular point in Cunard history during the 150th Anniversary voyage round Britain was more than enough to secure the interest of maritime historians and ship followers from around the world.

The balance of those one million spectators undoubtedly comprised former Cunarders and their families also keen to witness history being made, together with what appeared to be most of the population of the city and surrounding towns.

On the day, subsequent media reports suggest, many of these who turned out allowed their yearning hearts to rule their minds, powering the notion that the spectacle unfolding in front of them that day could become the norm; that Cunard could soon re-introduce a transatlantic service from Liverpool with QE2 the ship to run it.

That dream has not come true – but the spectacular events of Tuesday, 24 July, 1990 live forever in the minds of those who were there to enjoy the fun.

On board QE2, the experience being enjoyed by the 1,750 guests was masterminded by Hotel Manager John Duffy.

The Liverpudlian former pupil of St Francis Xavier's College and student at Cornell University, New York, became Cunard's youngest Hotel Manager when he was appointed in 1981. Before joining QE2, he had served on other great Cunarders including Queen Elizabeth, Carinthia, Carmania and Franconia.

He had not been alone in recognising the huge level of interest and the promotional value to be gained from a QE2 call at his home city.

"I felt that if QE2 went to Liverpool, other ships would follow – and that is what happened," he recalls. "It was a very emotional day. I had been asking the company for many, many years before that to take the ship to Liverpool because I knew it would be a very popular call."

As QE2 made her way majestically to her mid-Mersey anchorage in front of the Three Graces, the veteran Hotel Manager was on the Bridge. "I remember there being so many people. A reporter asked me why I thought there were so many spectators. That was an easy question to answer because I think virtually everybody in Liverpool has some connection with Cunard, whether it be an auntie, an uncle, a grandparent or a brother or a sister or a cousin. Whoever – somebody, sometime in the dim and distant has worked with Cunard, and that is why so many people turned out then and still do whenever a Cunarder calls at Liverpool."

In command that day was the late Captain Robin Woodall, *right*, a Wirral resident proud to be bringing QE2 to his home port for the first time.

During an interview in 2007 he recalled the excitement and challenges of the day.

"We had the Pilot on board, and I had spoken to him, obviously, about how the ship handled, and we came up to the Mersey Bar, and we sat waiting there for enough water to go over the Bar, and then once there was enough water we came up the channel.

"There was quite a fresh south easterly breeze, and as we came round the Crosby turn, I was looking over towards Crosby, and I remember it vividly to this day, all the sand was black. There is normally golden sand there, and I hadn't come into the river for many a long year. I hadn't been in that position to look over at Crosby for years and years. I remarked on this to the Pilot. I said it was a shame the mud had taken over from the sand, and he said: 'Oh no, that's people'. I looked through the binoculars, and sure enough

The late Captain Robin Woodall was in command of the QE2, top left, during her maiden call to Liverpool. Also pictured are Hotel Manager John Duffy and some of the ship's passengers

it was people thronging the beach to watch us arrive. And that was early in the day.

"The scenes at Crosby really set the tone for the day," recalled Captain Woodall.

"New Brighton was packed solid with people, and all the way up, Seacombe, Woodside and the Pier Head were packed with crowds and crowds of spectators.

"Then of course we came to anchor and that is when the fun started because we had a screaming flood tide beneath us with the wind in the opposite direction. I had said to the Pilot earlier on in the voyage when we were talking about how the ship handled, 'one thing this ship has got is four-wheel disc brakes, you know, she really can stop on a dime.' And when we started to swing the ship to come head to tide, and because of the tide underneath us, we were going quite quickly as we headed the bow in towards the Birkenhead dock entrance.

"The Pilot turned to me and said: 'You said this thing had good brakes. Prove it!' I did and we stopped, and we swung round quite happily and we anchored. Then the fun continued because, wind over tide, the ship would not settle. The wind was swinging her beam on to the tide, and then with the tide on the beam, she was dragging because the bottom of the Mersey is not good holding ground. It is

like soup. We had to keep the tugs on the ship despite being at anchor all morning and into the afternoon until the tide turned. The tugs just kept us stern into the wind, so we didn't have the tide dragging us. When the tide turned she was perfectly alright."

The conditions prevented the Captain from leaving the bridge to attend two important ceremonies ashore – the unveiling of a bust of Sir Samuel Cunard at the Merseyside Maritime Museum, and the consecration of plaques commemorating Cunard Line's War Dead at Liverpool Parish Church.

"I could not go because of the way the ship was behaving, so my Staff Captain went. He got as far as the Maritime Museum, but he could not get across to St Nicholas's because of the crowds. The place was just absolutely packed solid with people."

By late afternoon, the crowds on both sides of the river were still growing.

"By the evening, the breeze had dropped and we turned and swung to the flood and the ship lay perfectly well. She was perfectly comfortable," explained the Captain.

"Come sailing time, it was really quite dramatic, the spectacle, because we heaved up the anchor and just with a tug holding us we sat there. When the fireworks finished we

Right, Debbie Lowndes, the daughter of the late Captain Robin Woodall, pictured top, has fond memories of the day QE2 first came to Liverpool. Above, father and daughter are pictured with Debbie's mother, Eileen

Captain Tony Murphy, right, and Captain Robbie Quinn steer the Royal Iris out to meet the QE2

very kindly asked us to go on his boat and spend the day in the Mersey, soaking up the atmosphere, and joining the hundreds of other vessels that were going to be buzzing around QE2.

"This seemed like a great idea, so plans were made for a party of us to meet at Meols slipway early in the morning in order to be able walk out to John's boat at its mooring.

"The first person we met at the slip was also joining us, and I will never forget his first words to me, which were 'She's on the Bar'. I was so relieved as it meant that QE2 had arrived and was waiting for the tide to go up the Mersey without any mishaps on the way.

"As soon as the tide came in we left Meols, we were all so excited, and looking forward to seeing the ship in the Mersey.

"As we came around the point at New Brighton, we couldn't believe our eyes, as there was QE2, looking absolutely enormous, and from our perspective, dwarfing the Three Graces, and seemingly filling the Mersey. I nearly burst with pride to think that Dad was in command.

"The other thing that astounded everyone on board was the crowds thronging both sides of the river, there were thousands and thousands of people cheering and waving – a real carnival atmosphere. Despite the publicity, I don't think anyone had anticipated the crowds.

"Once the ship had dropped anchor we started to circle her, and popped the champagne corks on board our boat – time to party! It was fascinating watching the Ferries taking dignitaries to and from the ship. Unfortunately, Mum was left dockside for hours, and didn't get on board until later. Meanwhile, Dad was on the wing of the bridge watching the movement of the ship. He couldn't possibly have seen us, but we could see him. Next moment our boat's VHF radio crackled into life with 'CH7, CH7, CH7, this is Queen Elizabeth 2'. John immediately responded, much to the excitement from the passengers on board CH7, especially me.

"John told Dad where we were, and next minute he was waving at us from the bridge of the ship. I will never forget that moment, it gave us all such a buzz. I had a brief word with Dad, but he obviously had a lot on his plate, so we said our goodbyes.

"The news that evening was full of the QE2 in the Mersey, and it was great fun trying to spot us sailing round the ship. We had stayed in the Mersey as long as the tide would allow, savouring every moment, and then we went home. It was one of the most memorable days of my life."

set off. It was really quite dramatic – as soon as the display finished – whoosh – we'd gone. It was a fitting demonstration of QE2's speed. It had been a magnificent day!"

Captain Woodall's daughter, Debbie, was among dozens of spectators on a flotilla of small craft surrounding the ship in the Mersey.

She also has clear and happy memories of the day.

"The day dawned beautifully – sunny and dry. I was very nervous as my Dad was bringing QE2 – 'the world's greatest liner' – to his home port.

"It was the first time a Cunard passenger liner had been up the Mersey in a long time, and the publicity and hype had been incredible. Unfortunately, due to security issues, the only person allowed to join Dad on board was my Mum, Eileen, which, initially, disappointed me dreadfully.

"However, my then husband, Alan, was a member of Hoylake Lifeboat crew, and the coxswain, John McDermott,

The famous Mersey Ferries have played a prominent supporting role in the growth of Liverpool's cruise business. Whether tendering guests ashore from ships anchored in the river, or providing spectacular sightseeing trips during ship arrivals and firework departures, Ferries have been to the fore on every occasion of a Cunard call at Liverpool.

On the Bridge of the former Royal Iris on 24 July, 1990, was Captain Robbie Quinn.

"I was acting Master on the day QE2 first came to Liverpool. There was myself and another Captain who has since retired, on the old Royal Iris.

"We were heading out to Crosby to meet up with QE2, we'd taken at least three or four hundred people out to Crosby to meet her on the way in, and we'd set off at about 8 o'clock.

"We got off towards Crosby buoy at about 10 o'clock and that first sight of her coming out of the mist was pretty awesome. It was a lovely crisp morning with a mist, probably fog further out into Liverpool Bay, but coming in and where we were it was a mist.

"At first we could just see the funnel as she was coming along past Formby and you got the impression that she was just going to sail past Liverpool, but then as she turned the bend and came towards Crosby, then you got the full view of the bow and it was a pretty impressive sight.

"Our passengers on the ferry? Well, for want of a better word they were pretty dumbstruck! Even the people with cameras were looking in awe rather than taking pictures. They were just struck by the size of the ship.

"Then, as we got closer and closer, we could see the passengers on the open decks waving and we could even hear some of them cheering at us! We exchanged whistle salutes and that got them going. We then fell in and followed her down into the Mersey.

"Even looking ashore, to the promenade and the beaches, everywhere was absolutely heaving with people who had come out that day to see the QE2. It was incredible. And all day it was non-stop. More and more people coming to the river to see the ship, and we carried, easily, 20,000 passengers on our boats that day. It was amazing.

"The firework display when she left was spectacular too, and then when the display finished we were supposed to follow her out, but we had no chance with her speed. It was just a case of putting our engine on overdrive and holding on. She did what she could do and picked up speed fast, and she was away. It had been a fantastic day all round, absolutely fantastic."

How visit set stage for regular calls home

In the wake of Queen Elizabeth 2's triumphant maiden call at Liverpool in 1990, people across the city started to consider the opportunities and challenges in seeking to attract more cruise ships to the waterfront.

Two major stumbling blocks soon emerged. Firstly, there was nowhere to accommodate large ships alongside. The old Landing Stage close to Princes Dock, just to the north of the Three Graces, had been dismantled and removed in 1976.

In its place, a smaller and less versatile pontoon arrangement had been installed to handle Isle of Man Steam Packet traffic. Cruise lines would do all they could to avoid having to take their ships into the dock system – it took time and cost more money.

As Liverpool was to discover later, the surroundings created to handle high volume cargos inside the dock system were, frankly, an eyesore and not an environment to be enjoyed by passengers starting or ending their cruise holidays.

Without easy access to quaysides or landing stages, the only way visiting ships could call was by dropping anchor mid-river and tendering their guests ashore – another costly and time-consuming process undertaken by Mersey Ferries.

With its high and powerful tidal range, the Mersey was considered too hostile an environment for visiting ships to deploy their own tenders.

At times, visiting Masters and their Bridge Teams had

The Three Graces – The Royal Liver Building, Cunard Building and the Port of Liverpool Building – are pictured top in front of the old Landing Stage in 1959 and, above, the Crown Dynasty

their work cut out keeping their ships safe and stable, let alone running a tender service.

On countless occasions, visiting Captains have had to send their apologies and their deputies to previously arranged events on shore, such has been the challenge of a call at Liverpool. In tough conditions, and with anchors dragging in the mud, Captains are not able to leave their ships.

The second challenge facing the city was what to offer visiting passengers beyond a diet of football folklore and popular music heritage. Twenty plus years ago, the region's tourism sector, now referred to as the visitor economy, was far less diverse and as well-established as it is now, and the huge investment in major regeneration schemes along

the waterfront was yet to happen. For itinerary planners, Liverpool proved a bit of a misfit – the quirkiness of its offer, the challenge of the river and the additional cost of fuel to get a ship either south towards the sun, or north, around Scotland and north east towards Scandinavia and the Baltic, combining to keep the city off regular routes and out of the brochures.

For Cunard though, the spiritual home remained important. For a line established in the city in 1839, history and heritage were key strands and nowhere underpinned these two selling points better than Liverpool. So, when an unexpected series of events unfolded for Cunard early in 1993, Liverpool was handed a further opportunity. Under the ownership of the Trafalgar House conglomerate, Cunard formed a joint venture operation with Crown Cruise Line under which the modern Crown fleet was given Cunard funnel colours and other branding presence to form Cunard Crown.

The newest addition to this enlarged fleet was the 19,000-ton Crown Dynasty, nearing completion at a construction yard in Spain in the summer of 1993. When it became apparent that this new ship would be introduced into service by Cunard, the search started for ways to raise her profile. Arrangements had already been made for her to be christened in New York by former US First Lady Betty Ford.

Between leaving the shipyard and starting the Atlantic crossing, Crown Dynasty's schedule allowed for a call at Liverpool on 4 July – 153 years to the day since Britannia left the Mersey and headed for Boston. The opportunity was seized upon by Cunard's PR team and it was soon confirmed

that the newest ship to bear Cunard's name could be taken alongside at Pier Head.

This prospect sparked much discussion among Liverpool's movers and shakers about the feasibility of building a permanent facility to take ships alongside at Pier Head but it was to be another 14 years before this wish came true. The ship duly arrived in the Mersey after other promotional duties at Southampton. At the time, and long before the excesses of today's celebrity culture and social media frenzy, Cunard had identified the benefits of inviting TV personalities to its events.

This early and subtle form of endorsement paid dividends as national press picture editors were always looking out for famous faces to fill their pages. Thus, for Crown Dynasty's historic call at Liverpool, several cast members from the Manchester-based Granada TV production, Coronation Street accepted invitations to tour, be filmed and photographed and have lunch on board.

As the ship was due to sail to New York without passengers, the event also gave the crew a welcome chance to hone their skills with guests.

The guest list that Sunday afternoon also included Editors and Travel Editors from important regional newspapers across the north of England, ensuring plenty of profile for the new ship, Coronation Street – and for Liverpool. When Crown Dynasty left the Mersey that evening, she became the first Cunard ship since Franconia in 1968 to sail from Liverpool to New York – the historic crossing to be recreated 22 years later by Queen Mary 2 on 4 July, 2015.

From top left: First Lady Betty Ford with Queen Elizabeth, Liverpool's Landing Stage; holidaymakers headed for New Brighton in 1937 and, above, people returning from the Isle of Man make their way along the Landing Stage in 1951

1994

QUEEN ELIZABETH 2, WEDNESDAY, 31 AUGUST

"Cunard ships undoubtedly
do attract more attention
than other cruise liners
in the Mersey."

*Captain Bob Swift, Marine
Operations Manager, Liverpool
Cruise Terminal*

Four years elapsed between Queen Elizabeth 2's successful first call at Liverpool and her second. She returned to the Mersey on Wednesday, 31 August, 1994 and her arrival and progress to the anchorage off Pier Head was once more witnessed by tens of thousands of spectators on both sides of the river.

Mersey Ferries again provided a tender service to bring guests from the ship ashore.

Photographs and footage from the day underline the scale of the city's regeneration since then, and the development of the waterfront amenities and facilities which have now become an integral part of its appeal to visitors.

Visionaries in the city realised that the levels of investment being poured into developing and regenerating the waterfront were going to transform the look and feel of the Pier Head and the areas surrounding it.

Several major projects added weight to the arguments of those lobbying for more cruise business.

After decades of decline and decay, Liverpool was starting to recognise what needed to be done and which of its existing assets (including the Mersey and the Pier Head) were likely to prove even more valuable.

The lively and vibrant waterfront on to which cruise passengers now step was still some way off on the day of QE2's second call, and the challenges of holding the ship safely and securely in the middle of a river with such a high and fast tidal range remained. Despite the operational difficulties, nobody who witnessed the distinct and beautiful lines of the great liner in the Mersey in front of the famous Three Graces was less than moved by what they saw, and the popularity of Cunard calls amongst Liverpudlians was never in any doubt. Nor was the warmth of the welcome they gave visiting guests and crew.

Few people have as much knowledge and experience of the River Mersey as Bob Swift, appointed Marine Operations Manager at Liverpool Cruise Terminal in 2008 after 41 years as a Pilot on the Mersey, during which time he assisted more than 6,000 visiting vessels.

"Cunard ships undoubtedly do attract more attention than other cruise liners. I think probably because so many Liverpudlians and others from all over the North West of England have old family connections with Cunard," he says.

"Everyone appears to know that the Cunard Building was where transatlantic passenger trade started from, and that Cunard was for so long based here."

The veteran Pilot's experience is invaluable to the Cruise Liverpool team as well as to the operations teams at the cruise lines who plan where their ships sail and when.

He specialised as a River Pilot in handling large tankers and bulk carriers – experience he finds particularly useful as cruise ships visiting Liverpool are getting bigger each year.

"In the last 20 years or so of my career, I specialised in piloting large oil tankers and bulk carriers. Boarding these ships usually meant a long climb up a pilot ladder to the main deck," he recalls.

"Cruise ships are much easier to board, as they use the shell doors which are typically about 2.5m above the water, so it's a 1.0m step-up from a pilot launch.

"Handling a cruise liner differs from other ships in that they normally have more power, thrusters and propellers.

"They need this equipment to counter strong winds, as their side profile and thus 'windage' is enormous. They can often manage to manoeuvre with less tugs than conventional ships," Bob explains.

His experience has been enormously valuable to the team planning Cunard's 175th anniversary events on the Mersey, particularly the arrival of the Three Queens together in the Mersey on 25 May 2015.

"That promises to be a remarkable day," he says.

Twenty one years ago, as QE2 bid her farewell to Liverpool, few watching could have imagined that one day the entire Cunard fleet would be together on the Mersey.

1995

QUEEN ELIZABETH 2, SATURDAY, 2 SEPTEMBER

"Seeing QE2 in the Mersey in front of the
Cunard Building is a remarkable sight."

Captain Ronald W. Warwick, Master, Queen Elizabeth 2

Top, Captain Ron Warwick with his father, former Cunard Commodore William E. Warwick and, above, the view from aboard one of QE2's Bridge Wings

When Queen Elizabeth 2 made her third call at Liverpool on 2 September, 1995, an important chapter in the unique history of one family's close association with Cunard unfolded on the ship's Bridge Wing.

In Command that day was Captain Ron Warwick. On the ship's manifest appeared the name of his father, former Cunard Commodore William E. Warwick travelling as a passenger and enjoying the voyage in his retirement.

From their prime vantage point high above the water, and with QE2 now at her customary mid-river anchorage, father and son could look across to Birkenhead and see the rooftop of the former family home – the Royal Hotel at Rock Ferry.

William E. Warwick was QE2's first Captain, overseeing the ship's construction at the John Brown yard on the Clyde and her introduction into service.

His son remembers some of his father's early associations with QE2, in particular the period when the ship was being fitted out in Scotland.

"I was away a lot of the time and did not get to see my father much during the building. However, from time to time we met up and he would tell me what he had been up to. He had offices in Lower Regent Street, London, and South Western House in Southampton and a flat in Scotland so he was always on the move.

"He spent a lot of time investigating navigation equipment and visited the major manufacturers of the day.

"He sailed on cross channel ferries to assess the different types of radars.

"Once I remember him saying he had been trying out chairs all day to approve the suitability of them being used on board in inclement weather."

Captain Warwick has an extensive collection of QE2 memorabilia – but his set does not include an invitation to the launch.

He explains: "My father asked me if I would like to attend the launching but unfortunately I was going to be away at sea so could not attend. Many years later I wished I had accepted and then declined so that at least I would have had the invitation as a souvenir!"

A significant part of the QE2's successful history covers the period when this Merseyside father and son were each in Command.

Many years later, recalling the visit to Liverpool in September 1995, the proud son remembers standing with his father on the Bridge Wing.

"Having been brought up in Liverpool, this was a very special visit for him. He shared many of his reminiscences with me as we stood together on the Bridge.

"He could just see the place he was born, the Royal Hotel on the Birkenhead bank of the river. The ambition to take command was a goal I set myself when I joined the QE2 as a Junior Officer for the first time on 6 April, 1970, when she arrived in Southampton from New York.

"Over the years leading up to this time there had been changes of ownership and numerous changes of senior management each with their own ideas as how the company should be operated.

"Many of the ideas were good but along with them often came times of doubt as to whether Cunard would survive the commercial pressures of the passenger shipping industry.

"Often, before reaching Command, it was a question of keeping one's fingers crossed in the hope the ship would be still with us when the time came.

"To my good fortune, my luck was in and as we know, the

QE2 continued her remarkable career for many more years.

"Achieving command was a culmination of professional ambition and the personal hope that I could keep the QE2 'in the family' as a gesture of thanks for the support and encouragement I received from my father over the years.

"My father was a man of few words but the fact that he sailed with me as a passenger when I was in command meant that I had done alright in his eyes."

Later in his own distinguished career at sea, Captain Warwick was to follow further in his father's footsteps by being appointed Commodore of the Fleet whilst in command of Queen Mary 2, the longest, tallest and widest liner ever built. A ship whose size and scale would one day dominate the Mersey.

On 2 September, 1995, though that accolade belonged once again to QE2, the ship's Captain and his very important guest.

Captain Ron Warwick with a cake designed in the shape of the QE2

1996

QUEEN ELIZABETH 2, FRIDAY, 5 JULY

"For many people, QE2 conjures up
images of exotic voyages, excellent
service and fabulous food.
She certainly does that for me."

Carol Thatcher, writer and broadcaster

A quirk of scheduling meant Queen
Elizabeth 2's fourth visit to Liverpool took
place a day after the 156th anniversary of
Britannia sailing from the city on its first
North Atlantic crossing.

Quite how or why the opportunity was missed is unclear,
but it was Friday, 5 July, 1996, rather than the 4 July that
year, when the most famous ship in the world returned to the
Mersey for the day.

Her arrival and presence in the river proved as big a hit as
ever with spectators, and guests returning to their ship after
trips ashore reported the warmest of welcomes.

As well as tendering duties, Mersey Ferries also ran a day-
long schedule of sightseeing cruises, giving several hundred
of those lucky enough to board the little boats a rare chance
to see the QE2 at close quarters as she sat at in the middle
of the river.

QE2 made history and broke records pretty much
everywhere she went.

She was built at the John Brown Shipyard on the Clyde
in Scotland and was known only as "Job Number 736" until
she was officially launched by Her Majesty Queen Elizabeth
II in September 1967 – and she was the last Atlantic liner to
be built on the Clyde.

In 1982, she was requisitioned by the UK Government for
service in the Falklands Campaign, and so joined the ranks
of the great Cunarders called upon to serve the country in
times of conflict.

She had the capacity to carry as many as 1,778 passengers
and more than 1,000 crew. The liner was almost 1,000 feet
long (963ft) and 105ft wide and had a top speed of more
than 32 knots – her propulsion system capable of moving
her at faster speeds backwards that most ships could manage
forwards.

Clockwise from top: HMS Sheffield crew members aboard the QE2 as they make their way home from the Falklands; lunch in the QE2's Columbia Restaurant, which was turned into a dining room for servicemen during the Falklands War, and two young girls wave goodbye as the ship leaves Southampton

Left, QE2 at the quayside at Southampton after her return from the South Atlantic with 700 survivors from HMS Antelope, Ardent and Coventry. She arrived to a jubilant welcome from families and friends gathered at the waterfront. Below, work being carried out on the deck of the QE2 to convert it into a helipad for a Sea King helicopter, and field beds arranged in what was the casino, which served as overspill accommodation for servicemen

"A well-designed ship, with sleek flowing lines, a sharply raked bow and well-rounded profile, she looked a picture in the Mersey."

Liverpool Echo correspondent

1999

ROYAL VIKING SUN, SATURDAY, 4 SEPTEMBER

Although its history and heritage are rooted in the provision of the North Atlantic service linking Europe with the New World, Cunard, through its various ownerships of the 1980s and 1990s, became as aware as any operator of the huge potential for growth in the cruise sector of the leisure market.

It was against such a background that many big operators seeking to increase their capacity in the market (by making more cabins available on more ships bearing their brands) rode a merry-go-round of ship sales, transfers and acquisitions.

The peaks and troughs of the market cycle meant some cruise operators were doing well and looking to increase their offer whist others — most notably major conglomerates with interests outside passenger shipping — were looking to divest cruise ship interests.

For those at the top of this wave, buying a good ship was often a more attractive proposition than commissioning a new build. It certainly meant revenue would flow more quickly.

Thus, in June 1994, Cunard announced it has purchased the Royal Viking brand, and its flagship Royal Viking Sun, from the huge Norwegian Kloster Group in a deal reportedly worth $170m.

The addition to the Cunard offer was greeted as a good deal by industry watchers at the time.

Royal Viking had established itself as a high-end brand with a good reputation for quality and service. The ship itself attracted a loyal customer base (many of whom referred to their favourite ship simply as "RVS") and, since entering service in 1988, had been independently rated the world's Number 1 ship every year.

As Cunard Royal Viking Sun, and with the familiar Cunard brick red livery on her funnel, the ship made a one-day call at Liverpool on 4 September, 1999, dropping anchor mid-river throughout the warm, sunny late summer day.

Following the acquisition of Cunard by Carnival Corporation, Royal Viking Sun soon found herself once again on a journey to a different operator (albeit one within the Carnival family) and was assigned to Seabourn as Seabourn Sun before transferring again within the Carnival brand portfolio to become Holland American Line's Prinsendam.

1999

"Flags waving like crazy, the Red Ensign rising up the mast amidst a dazzling display of fireworks. Golly, how we cheered!"

Dame Beryl Bainbridge

Modern ship-naming ceremonies have become events capable of swallowing huge budgets and appearing to need casts of hundreds.

Cunard delivered what is widely regarded by many as the finest such show ever staged when Her Majesty the Queen named Queen Mary 2 in Southampton on 8 January, 2004.

The ship of superlatives required a launch event to match.

Few of the 2,000-plus guests seated in the specially-built dockside auditorium at the Queen Elizabeth II Terminal could believe the scale and spectacle of what they witnessed that winter's afternoon.

Yet five years earlier, at the last naming of a Cunard ship, everything had been a lot different.

In December 1999 the final pieces of a rebrand and restructure, initiated following the acquisition of Cunard by the huge US-based Carnival Corporation, were nearing completion.

Under the directions of the new owners, Cunard was to operate two vessels, its flagship and legendary Queen Elizabeth 2 and the former Vistafjord which was to be renamed Caronia.

Almost a decade has passed since QE2 made her first, spectacular call at Liverpool. In the intervening years her returns to the Mersey continued to generate huge interest and command attention. No opportunity to remind the world that Liverpool was Cunard's spiritual home was ever

The renaming and rededication of

CARONIA

Friday 10 December 1999
The Pierhead, Liverpool

Order of Service

wasted. Thus, the city was chosen to host the renaming and rededication of Caronia.

The announcement prompted great excitement and anticipation in Liverpool, not least because it was intended that Caronia would berth alongside at the Princes Landing Stage, within sight of the Cunard Building.

If all went to plan, the latest addition to the Cunard fleet would occupy an historic stretch of the Liverpool waterfront.

It was from here, on 30 January 1968, that the last Cunard ship to leave Liverpool with passengers bound for New York departed. The Franconia went via Bermuda marking what Cunard only ever described as the "suspension" of its transatlantic services from Liverpool!

Further history had been made on the same stretch of water on 4 July 1993, during the call to Liverpool by Cunard Crown Dynasty.

The stage was therefore set for the spiritual home to host the start of another new chapter in Cunard history.

As well as exciting the historians, those lucky enough to be invited to participate in the ceremony soon had their own reasons to be excited – not to mention a little apprehensive.

Following the formalities of the ceremony and a celebratory dinner on board, Caronia and her guests would sail from Liverpool bound for Southampton. The prospect of that passage in December, with a poor weather forecast, stirred seasoned travellers.

Caronia duly arrived in Liverpool from the Lloyd-Werft shipyard in Bremerhaven, Germany, in the early hours of Friday, 10 December 1999 and spent several hours anchored in the river before coming alongside at the Landing Stage.

Around 600 Cunard guests "checked in" for their mini cruise to Southampton at a waterfront hotel before being ushered to the Isle of Man Steam Packet Company passenger facilities to prepare for boarding before Luncheon.

Preparations for the ceremony continued throughout the afternoon, including the building of a small covered platform on the Landing Stage and rehearsals for the Liverpool Philharmonic Concert Orchestra and Singers together with Master of Ceremonies, Michael Buerk, the BBC journalist.

The renaming was to have been performed by Mrs Madeleine Arison, wife of Carnival Corporation Chairman and Chief Executive Officer Micky Arison, but illness on the day meant her place was taken by Mrs Pamela Conover, Cunard's Chief Operating Officer.

Former Cunard Steward John Prescott – by then Secretary of State for the Environment, Transport and the Regions – was on hand to raise the Red Ensign, reflecting the ship's new registry. In his brief address to guests he famously referred to Cunard President Larry Pimentel as Larry "Pimpernel".

His difficulties with the names of senior Carnival and Cunard executives continued five years later during an event on board QE2 when he referred to Micky Arison as "Mr Harrison".

Above, John Prescott hoists the Red Ensign on the newly-named Caronia, berthed at the Pier Head in Liverpool, where a large crowd gathered to watch the ceremony. The former Deputy Prime Minister is also pictured speaking above right, with Master of Ceremonies and BBC journalist Michael Buerk on the left

The renaming and rededication were completed well within the hour and guests re-embarked in an orderly fashion as the choir sang carols and thoughts turned towards the celebratory dinner.

The decision had been taken to move Caronia off the berth during the evening to a position in the river where she could drop anchor before what promised to be a spectacular firework departure just after 2200 hrs.

This manoeuvre was agreed by the ship and port officials after an outcrop of rock protruding from the mud of the Mersey had been discovered close to the Landing Stage. Fears had been expressed for the safety of Caronia's hull as the tide fell.

As guests on board enjoyed their gala dinner, the weather outside was worsening with heavy, squally rain falling on tens of hundreds of spectators waiting patiently for the send-off.

Their patience and resilience was rewarded with a spectacular firework display and soon Caronia was off on a course that would take her along the North Wales coast to Anglesey where she would alter course to head for St George's Channel.

The passage was horrendous. Severe gales troubled Caronia and her guests throughout the early hours of Saturday morning and by the time day broke the storm was even more severe. Some failed to stir from their cabins for breakfast. Many of those who did thought better of it. Chaotic but comical scenes unfolded during the annual Cunard Christmas Press Lunch taking place in a restaurant at the highest point of the pitching, rolling ship.

Revised forecasts offered little hope for those already laid low. The first prospect of any improvement was deemed by many to be at the point off Cornwall and the Isles of Scilly when Caronia would enter the English Channel and take a course with the battering winds on her stern rather than on her starboard side as they had been since North Wales.

That turning point came too late for many guests whose experience had been ruined by the mountainous seas. By Sunday morning, with Caronia fast alongside at Southampton (in the shadow of her "new" sister, QE2) calmness finally prevailed. Those who were not weary and exhausted readied themselves for a special Luncheon on board QE2 – herself fresh from a £30m refit.

Nobody who witnessed the naming of the Caronia at the Pier Head will ever forget the simple yet moving ceremony. Nor will the event, and all that followed, ever be forgotten by those who sailed from Liverpool that night.

2000

"The ambition to take command was a goal
I set myself when I joined Queen Elizabeth 2
as a Junior Officer for the first time on 6 April, 1970."

Captain Ronald W. Warwick, Master, Queen Elizabeth 2

Queen Elizabeth 2 returned to the Mersey on 13 July, 2000, making her fifth call at Liverpool and marking the 10th anniversary of her first triumphant visit.

Her Liverpool fan club remained as loyal as ever and, despite her early arrival at the Bar and unseasonal weather, crowds once again gathered on the beaches at Crosby and New Brighton; the Mersey Ferries were full and a flotilla of small craft followed her stately progress to the mid-river anchorage.

An air of calm prevailed on the Bridge under the command of Captain Ron Warwick – proud to once again be bringing the most famous liner in the world to his home port of Liverpool.

A Morse code message flashed to a cargo ship in the mid-1960s was to spark a life-long interest in QE2 for the Liverpool-born Captain.

He was serving as Second Mate on the Jamaica Producer when his father was appointed Master Designate of QE2.

"The radio officer told me he had read about the appointment when he received the daily news by Morse code," he explains.

"On my return to London, I collected all the press cuttings about my father and subsequently became interested in the ship itself. Ever since, and up to the present day, I have kept and filed cuttings and articles about QE2."

The cuttings in his unique collection chart the remarkable history of the ship brought into service by his father and of which he took command in 1990.

He recalls vividly two defining moments in his association with the ship – the first time he saw her at sea and the first time he boarded her as a guest of his father.

"I first saw QE2 when she was carrying out some sea trials

Captain Ron Warwick at the controls of the QE2 as it arrives in Liverpool

in the English Channel. I was outward bound from London on another ship and our Radio Officer heard QE2 so he sent a message for me. An hour or so later the QE2 came up on our stern and passed us a mile or so off at full speed. It was a very impressive sight," he remembers.

His first visit to his father's Command was in Kingston, Jamaica.

"I went on board for the first time when she was on her inaugural winter cruise season and called at Kingston. At the time I was also in port on my ship. Compared to my 18-year-old cargo ship, she was a palace and I remember being quite overwhelmed by the technology on the Bridge and the magnificence of the interior décor.

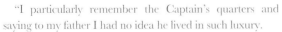

"I particularly remember the Captain's quarters and saying to my father I had no idea he lived in such luxury.

"I was so impressed by the ship that I decided the only way to go to sea was on a liner. A few months later I applied for a position with Cunard Line and joined the company in April 1970 with the goal, and a lot of hope, of being the Captain of QE2 one day."

Two decades later his ambition was fulfilled and he clearly relished the emotional return to Liverpool with QE2 a further ten years later.

"One of the most attractive features about Liverpool is the fact that we can be accommodated in the heart of the city. In many ports around the world, QE2 has to berth in the

Left, musician
Elton John, with
then-wife Renate
in 1984, arriving
in Southampton
following a world
voyage on QE2

industrial areas of the harbour. To be near the architectural heart of the city on the World Heritage Site waterfront is a fitting place for a Cunard Queen to be," he says.

In the days before Liverpool's cruise berth was available, he recalls the challenges of running a tender service to ferry guests from the ship to the shore and back as QE2 sat mid-river in front of the Cunard Building.

The weather during the morning of 13 July 2000 remained poor, adding to the complexity of the task faced by the crew of the Mersey Ferry providing the tender.

"Any port where we have to use tenders requires extra care and diligence form our crew," explained the Captain. "Liverpool was often more demanding because of the strong tidal stream and the fact that the holding ground of the river bed is not ideal for such a large liner, and dragging of the anchor is likely to occur, especially when the tide turns."

As the day went on more and more spectators gathered on both sides of the river to view the spectacle. Also impressed by the sight of the ship in Liverpool that summer's day was regular passenger Sir Elton John, whose helicopter flew over the liner on its way to a concert at a riverside arena.

"Seeing QE2 in the Mersey in front of the Cunard Building is a remarkable sight," the Captain pointed out. "QE2's visits to the Mersey have always served to reinforce the bond between Cunard and the city," he says.

And 13 July 2000 did just that.

2003

"Such an elegant Cunarder...
and she looks right at home in the Mersey."

Liverpool Daily Post correspondent

Four years after her naming and rededication at Liverpool, Caronia returned to the Mersey to make her second and final call as a Cunard ship.

Her acquisition and branding as a Cunarder in 1999 had proved a popular decision with cruise passengers for whom she was soon established as a popular choice.

After the drama of her arrival in the city in 1999 and concerns about an outcrop of rock off the landing stage where she eventually tied up alongside, no risks were taken during the second call and she took up the familiar position at anchor.

The day's tendering operation once again proved to be a major challenge for Caronia's Bridge Team led by Captain Nick Bates and the Mersey Ferry crews.

For a long period during the day, the speed of the tidal flow, and other prevailing conditions, made it impossible for the Mersey Ferry to get alongside Caronia safely enough for passengers to transfer between the two vessels.

Eventually, a combination of repositioning the ship and calmer conditions allowed tendering to resume, although some guests who had witnessed the Ferry's attempts to get alongside from Caronia's upper decks changed their minds about going ashore.

Tales of the morning's adventures relayed by returning guests only served to convince them they had made the right decision to admire Liverpool from the comfort of their ship rather than admire their ship from the Pier Head.

Designed, built and launched as the Vistafjord at Swan Hunter's Tyneside yard in 1973, the ship bore classic liner styling and profile, perfectly observed during her time in the Mersey.

Her original specification used excellent quality materials and after entering service with Cunard in 1983 standards were painstakingly maintained with Caronia's range of itineraries, and the quality of on-board services and amenities, proving enormously popular with guests.

Her final call at Liverpool came as the finishing touches were being put to the new Queen Mary 2, the arrival on the scene of the mighty new flagship prompting another shuffle of the Cunard pack which saw Caronia sold to Saga Cruises in 2004.

Caronia pictured during her second visit to Liverpool and, above, as the Vistafjord, before she became a Cunard liner

2004

QUEEN ELIZABETH 2, MONDAY, 31 MAY
AND MONDAY, 30 AUGUST

"I can remember the Blue Meanie. I have met some
interesting people in my time but he was unique."

Captain Ian McNaught, Master, Queen Elizabeth 2

After an absence from the Mersey lasting almost four years, Queen Elizabeth 2 was scheduled to make two calls at Liverpool in 2004, each falling during Bank Holiday weekends in May and August when the potential for further large crowds to witness the spectacle was even greater than normal.

The city was still without its cruise facility, meaning the majority of vessels visiting for the day without entering the lock and dock systems were required to drop anchor off the Pier Head and invite their guests to board a Mersey Ferry tender ashore.

Those overseeing these operations freely admit the Mersey is a challenging environment in which to run such a tender service and, privately at least, some observers suggested QE2's absence for four years was

partly down to the mid-river anchorage. Some even believed it was an attempt to hasten the torturous and time-consuming process which had swamped the project to build a proper berthing facility.

Quite how either theory squares with the decision to allow QE2 to call mid-river twice within three months is anyone's guess. Like any absence, it appeared to make the hearts grow fonder and huge crowds again turned out throughout the first of the 2004 calls.

The second call that year coincided with the city's annual homage to its four home-grown lads who shook the world — The Beatles.

QE2 guests stepping ashore at Pier Head from their Mersey Ferry Tender Service found themselves immersed in the unique atmosphere and experience of the Mathew Street Festival and, a little further across the city centre, at the finale of that year's International Beatle Week extravaganza

The Blue Meanie, the music-hating creature which featured in the Beatles' film Yellow Submarine, makes an appearance during the 2004 Mathew Street Festival, an event which also featured 12-foot-tall puppets of the Fab Four, pictured far right, and coincided with a visit from QE2

hosted for the most part at the Adelphi Hotel. In its far grander heyday the Adelphi was a pivotal part of Cunard's transatlantic service and provided guests about to embark their liner with a night's rest after reaching the port, or for those disembarking inbound services, a further respite before any onward journey.

Few if any of the QE2 guests coming ashore that day could be surprised by the commotion being created around the Beatles since they had been joined during their voyage to Liverpool by one of the notorious Blue Meanies, the army of allegedly fierce, music-hating creatures featured in the Beatles' 1968 film Yellow Submarine.

The sea-going Meanie had availed himself of all of QE2's facilities during his passage to Liverpool, adopting the ship's renowned Chart Room bar as its base.

Cunard Captains are well versed in the protocols of welcoming and hosting VIPs aboard their ships – especially those in command of QE2, as Captain Ian McNaught recalls: "I can remember the Blue Meanie. I have met some interesting people in my time but he was unique.

"Everybody has a story to tell whether they are famous or not. I can remember sharing a cup of tea after dinner one evening on the Bridge Wing with Buzz Aldrin, and we were looking at the sky. I said: 'Doesn't the moon look wonderful this evening?' and he turned round and replied: 'Yes it does. I've been there you know'."

The Blue Meanie relaxes on board QE2 while, right, he entertains Captain Ian McNaught and has a drink at the bar. Also pictured is the Adelphi Hotel – which was often a port of call for Cunard passengers

2007

QUEEN ELIZABETH 2, FRIDAY, 21 SEPTEMBER

"To be able to go alongside a berth in front of those three wonderful buildings at Liverpool's Pier Head was a huge thing to celebrate that day."

Captain Ian McNaught, Master, Queen Elizabeth 2

After years of false starts and funding wrangles, Liverpool finally built its long-awaited cruise liner facility during 2006/2007.

The stakes were high for the city and those backing the project, not least because of the challenges presented by the vast tidal range of the Mersey.

The requirement was to be able to handle large, modern cruise ships outside the dock system by providing a vast, floating landing stage to which visiting ships could secure themselves whilst remaining in the river at all states of the tide.

With a ship on one side of the stage, the opposite was to be connected to the river wall by two link span bridges fitted with intricate hinge mechanisms to cope with the rise and fall of the tide. The concrete pontoon sections of the stage were themselves attached via a set of moveable "collars" to a series of piles sunk deep into the river bed. The collars allowed the stage to float up and down the piles with the ebb and flow of the tide.

Construction of the pontoons had taken place in a dry dock with a schedule agreed for them to be towed into position by tugs and for the collars on each section to be secured to the piles. Final pre-installation checks were carried out in another dry dock at the Cammell Laird shipyard at Birkenhead before tugs brought the sections across the river to be put into place.

Construction and engineering teams worked round the clock to meet the deadline for the official opening of the facility on 21 September, 2007.

The shore side formalities were performed by His Royal Highness the Duke of Kent. On the water, opening ceremony duties fell to no lesser ship than Queen Elizabeth 2.

The British merchant flagship's call at Liverpool that day formed part of a spectacular lap of honour around the British Isles to mark QE2's 40th anniversary.

At her home port of Southampton, and with celebrations

on board in full swing, QE2 let go her ropes on the afternoon of Saturday, 15 September, 2007 to start the special voyage which would include a maiden call to the Tyne, a visit to South Queensferry on the Firth of Forth and a call to the Clyde before all eyes fell on Liverpool at dawn on Friday, 21 September.

Many on board had set their alarms early to be in position on the open decks for what promised to be a memorable arrival at Liverpool. Sadly, low cloud and heavy rain greeted them as they made their way to vantage points around the liner.

Conditions that morning in Liverpool were a stark contrast to the previous day in Greenock on the Clyde. There, the RAF Red Arrows had presented their unique contribution to the celebration voyage with a stunning display beneath clear skies, and QE2's whistle was blown for 40 seconds from precisely the time she was launched into the river from John Brown's shipyard.

His Royal Highness the Duke of Kent, right, and Lord Mayor Paul Clark unveil the commemorative plaque to declare the City of Liverpool Cruise Liner Terminal open

Despite the rain and poor visibility, hundreds of guests were outdoors as QE2 crossed the Mersey Bar. They were unable to see car headlights flashing and camera flash guns popping from the car parks and beaches at Crosby and New Brighton and all along the Wirral promenade to the Mersey Ferry Terminal at Seacombe.

At the best forward facing vantage point available to guests on board, spectators huddled for shelter beneath QE2's bridge, straining to recognise shapes emerging on the waterfront. The only sound they could hear was of the motors driving wipers on the Bridge windows.

Shortly after 7am QE2 was alongside the new City of Liverpool Cruise Liner Facility where final preparations for the rest of the official opening ceremony were in hand.

The Royal Party duly arrived and HRH, assisted by the Lord Mayor of Liverpool Councillor Paul Clark, unveiled the commemorative plaque to declare the landing stage open.

The short ceremony went largely unnoticed by Cunard guests drying out on board the ship. For them the undoubted highlight of the day was still to come – a special 40th Anniversary Concert to celebrate the remarkable QE2 story in words and music at Liverpool Cathedral.

The concert featured renowned artists Lesley Garrett and Nicky Spence together with the Royal Liverpool Philharmonic Orchestra and Choir, the Liverpool Cathedral Choir, the band of the Scots Guards and Professor Ian Tracy playing the organ. The conductor was Anthony Inglis.

The musical programme was interspersed with short addresses to the audience including one from broadcaster and writer Carol Thatcher who was sailing on board QE2.

She told guests in the Cathedral: "For many people, QE2 conjures up images of exotic voyages, excellent service and fabulous food.

"She certainly does that for me. But she also conjures up

for me memories of her role in the Falklands War, which was a tense and turbulent time for my family – as it was for many others.

"I well remember surprise being expressed when my mother sanctioned the requisition of QE2 for service in the war. There was concern that the loss of such a notable British icon, such a high-profile symbol of what is best about Britain, would be a huge blow to public morale.

"And certainly my mother is on record as saying that she never had so many sleepless nights as Prime Minister as she did during the weeks the liner was journeying to the South Atlantic.

"But, of course, there was no choice. No other ship could have carried so many, so far, so fast.

"Few of us will forget her emotional return on 11 June, 1982, when she sailed into Southampton bearing the survivors of HMS Coventry, Antelope and Ardent and was saluted by The Queen Mother on board the Royal Yacht Britannia.

"And few will forget the day she sailed out of Southampton, 12 May, 1982 – having been converted in just eight days into a troopship, and carrying to the theatre of war the 3,000 troops of the Fifth Infantry Brigade – made up of the Welsh Guards, the Gurkha Rifles and, of course, the magnificent men of the Scots Guards."

Her final words were the cue for the Band of the Scots Guards to march into the Cathedral playing Sailing.

QE2's Master Captain Ian McNaught climbed the pulpit to give the final address.

He said: "Today, together, we have celebrated the long and extraordinary life of a great ocean liner. An ocean liner which was conceived and planned here in Liverpool.

"So far, QE2 has visited Liverpool – which was Cunard's home for 128 years – eight times.

"But the next time, the ninth time, will be the last time. After that, she will not pass this way again."

Tears trickled down the cheeks of many present as the Concert reached a crescendo and Captain McNaught's words reminded them QE2 was soon to leave Liverpool forever.

HAPPY 40TH BIRTHDAY

FROM CREW

40TH ANNIVERSARY 1967-2007

AND PASSENGERS TO YOU

MIND YOUR HEAD

QUEEN ELIZABETH 2

CUNARD

Terminal's opening 'marked the start of a new chapter'

Captain Ian McNaught, now Deputy Master, Trinity House, recalls the call to Liverpool well.

"The new Cruise Terminal…oh yes, I remember the rain as we arrived, but really, to be able to go alongside a berth in front of those three wonderful buildings at Liverpool's Pier Head was a huge thing to celebrate, and it has opened the way for Liverpool to become a really successful port of call for the cruise industry to enjoy.

"Anchoring in the Mersey is always a challenge, there is quite a strong ebb and flood there, so it was never easy and required good old fashioned seamanship to get it right.

"Running passengers to and from the shore using the ferries was always, how shall I say, interesting, but with the great skills of the ferry Captains, we usually managed it without too much drama, always interesting days though.

"In that respect the arrival of QE2 alongside that day to launch the new terminal marked the start of a new chapter for Liverpool."

Cruise Liverpool Marine Operations Manager Bob Swift

Joining Captain McNaught and the QE2 Bridge Team for the arrival in the Mersey that day was Liverpool River Pilot Bob Swift. He recalls the tension as the ship made its passage from New Brighton to the berth at Princes Parade.

"Two tugs were delayed in the Gladstone dock, they were on a Hapag-Lloyd container ship and various things about the job caused the delay.

"Thank goodness the tug Trafalgar was already in the river and met and made fast to the stern of the QE2 just at the entrance to the river.

"We then did all that we could to kill time to allow the other tugs to join us but it was difficult. The QE2 at that time only had one bow thruster in use which was restricted in its power. It was running constantly to Starboard most of the way from New Brighton to try to counter the strong Westerly wind on the approach to the Cruise Terminal.

"Each time the Trafalgar hauled the stern up to the West the force of the wind overpowered the effect of the bow thruster, and the bow turned to Port. We then had to stop the Trafalgar and use the ship's engines, with rudder hard to Starboard to kick the bow back up to the West.

"As QE2 got close to the berth we decided to approach with the presumption that we would land alongside with just the stern tug fast.

"We realised that the tugs Waterloo and Gladstone were off their other job, out of the Lock and on the way down to us.

"Captain McNaught and I were out on QE2's Port bridge wing about to drop alongside, hopefully as flat and with as little weight as possible, and we could not see the other two tugs.

"The Waterloo arrived at great speed and managed to put a tow rope up onto the foredeck when we were about five metres from the berth. It was the quickest 'make fast' ever.

"This additional line meant the Waterloo was able to counter the effect of last minute weight to the West with the Trafalgar and drop QE2 gently into position onto the berth.

"The gangway position on the berth had to be precise – we had a tolerance of just four inches!

"The tug Gladstone arrived shortly after the Waterloo, took position amidships, and gently pushed in as requested and held QE2 alongside the berth until all mooring lines were out.

"I have always had the greatest respect for the skills of Liverpool Tug Masters and their crews. This day's tug work was exceptional."

2008

QUEEN ELIZABETH 2, FRIDAY, 3 OCTOBER

"I was always amazed by the numbers who were
there to greet us and see us off…
I really loved that ship and all that went with her."

Captain Ian McNaught, Master, Queen Elizabeth 2

Since the tumultuous reception she received on the Mersey in July 1990, Queen Elizabeth 2 had continued to attract tens of thousands of spectators every time she called at Liverpool. But on Friday, 3 October, 2008 it was time to say goodbye.

This was to be her last call at Cunard's spiritual home. In a little more than a month after this visit, the ship would leave her home port of Southampton for the last time.

There had been high demand for places on board her farewell round-Britain voyage from the moment it went on sale. QE2 regulars were as keen to bid their farewells as were those who realised time was running out to experience life on board the most famous ocean liner in history.

For everyone fortunate to secure a place on board, the call at Liverpool promised to be the highlight of a very memorable voyage.

Her previous visits to Liverpool had become the stuff of legend among devotees of QE2. From the dramatic arrival in the Mersey and the approach to the city's historic waterfront, to the packed promenades and crowded Mersey Ferries, Liverpool's welcome for QE2 was always known to be something special.

After arriving for the first time on that scorching hot July day in 1990, QE2 had not always been blessed with fine weather at Liverpool.

For her final visit though the weather gods prevailed and she made her way over the Bar under blue skies and in bright autumn sunshine.

Sharp-eyed spectators with a knowledge of maritime tradition immediately noticed a distinctly different feature about the ship on this arrival.

Flying proudly from the mast was the QE2's Paying Off Pennant – a specially commissioned, 39 foot long flag, with every 12 inches representing one year of the liner's service with Cunard. Paying Off Pennants are flown immediately prior to the ship leaving service. QE2's was the longest in Cunard history.

During the day of functions and festivities which was to follow QE2's safe arrival, members of the ship's company gathered to bear a replica of the Pennant down the central aisle of Liverpool Cathedral during a Commemorative Concert arranged by Cunard.

The pennant was presented to one-time Cunard steward and former Deputy Prime Minister John Prescott, who in turn presented it to the then Lord Mayor of the City, Councillor Steve Rotheram, now Member of Parliament for

Liverpool Walton. During the concert he addressed guests with the following words: "Even though Cunard left the City of Liverpool forty years ago, it has never really gone away.

"Represented still by that solid central edifice of our world-famous Three Graces, known even now as the Cunard Building, Cunard is woven into the fabric of this city.

"Today, forty years on, everybody knows somebody who used to work for Cunard – or who still does.

"And I think the reverse is also true: wherever in the world Cunard's office may be – and it has been in a number of different places since leaving here – the company's heart will always be Liverpool.

"And so it gives me particular pride to welcome all of you – be you QE2 passengers, QE2 crew or Liverpudlians with a fondness for Cunard – to this celebration of the life of the most famous ship in the world. A ship which was conceived and designed here in Liverpool.

The QE2 sailing majestically past Crosby, opposite, while spectators catch a close-up view of the legendary vessel

"Cunard's time in Liverpool, although it lasted 128 years, is gone; QE2's time as an ocean-going liner, although the longest-serving in history, is almost gone. But in our hearts, both will live on.

"So, although 'the day Thou gavest, Lord, is ended, the dawn leads on another day'."

The then Dean of Liverpool, The Very Reverend Justin Welby, now Archbishop of Canterbury, told guests: "All earthly things must change; all earthly things must pass. And even though QE2 seems to be a permanent feature of British life, she too must move on. So this, her ninth visit to Liverpool, is her last.

"But she will be remembered for generations to come, and those who are now young will talk to their grandchildren of the times they saw the most famous ship in the world anchored in the Mersey. All of us will remember QE2, and some may even visit her in her new role in Dubai; even though she will still exist, she will have changed, and we never be able to recapture fully what we see today.

"As A E Houseman so beautifully described the memory of things gone:

Into my heart an air that kills
From you far country blows
What are those blue remembered hills,
What spires, what farms are those
"That is the land of lost content,
I see it shining plain,
The happy highways where I went
And cannot come again.

"But though we may be wistful today at the final passing of this great liner, we will look to new horizons next year when QE2's successor, Queen Mary 2, arrives in the Mersey for the first time. For as things change, and as they pass, so life is renewed. While we are right to be sad in life from time to time, we must have faith in what is to come.

"Faith, after all, is God's Amazing Grace."

Retired Cunard Captain Robin Woodall, Master of QE2 during her first visit to Liverpool in 1990, was invited to read at the Concert, telling guests: "Many people here today, and many more throughout the world, have walked beside QE2 on every step of her long and eventful life.

"They have been there with her, in spirit if not in the flesh, at every defining moment. Defining moments which QE2, supremely well built, supremely beautiful, supremely fast, has met with grace and dignity.

"They have swelled at her triumphs – the emotional return from the Falklands, the heart-stopping welcomes in Sydney and Liverpool and the triumphant 40th Anniversary voyage – and they have felt for her under attack from uncharted rocks, or from botched refits or from would-be terrorists.

"They have walked beside her through days of cloud and sunshine, joy and tears.

"No ship has had so many walk beside her for so long or for so far through the passing years

Opposite, staff at the Panoramic 34 restaurant at Liverpool's West Tower watch QE2 sail past as the ship prepares to berth at the Pier Head, above. Below left, the then Dean of Liverpool the Very Rev. Justin Welby, addressing guests at the Commemorative Concert

"And now all of us walk beside her as she travels to the land of dreams."

As the Pennant Party started their procession from the vast Cathedral's West Doors, the Royal Liverpool Philharmonic Orchestra and the Cathedral Choir, directed by Anthony Inglis, performed Fauré's In Paradisum.

Row by row, the ship's passengers and civic guests invited by Cunard on behalf of the City of Liverpool, turned their heads to observe the procession make its way towards the presentation.

It proved to be the first of many emotional moments for those present – the length of the flag serving to remind everyone how long QE2 had been both the flagship of the British Merchant fleet and an icon of British style.

Emotions were further stirred by the appearance of Falklands War veteran Simon Weston who had sailed to the South Atlantic on board QE2 after she was requisitioned by the Ministry of Defence to join the Task Force.

The former Welsh Guardsman was severely injured after he and comrades transferred from QE2 to the troop carrier Sir Galahad and it came under attack.

In a striking and fitting tribute to both Simon Weston's bravery and QE2's war service, the Band of the Welsh Guards played Sailing as they marched into the Cathedral and down the aisle.

As the Commemorative Concert drew towards a crescendo, Captain Ian McNaught, Master of QE2, made his way to the pulpit.

He said: "QE2 was born in Clydebank; but she was conceived in Liverpool. The decision to build her was made here; the struggle to finance her was coordinated here; that beautiful classic profile first emerged from a drawing board here; the iconic funnel was shaped here; her revolutionary technology was determined here; the vibrant, unorthodox interiors were approved right here. Here, in Liverpool on the Pier Head.

"The people of Liverpool have as much right to claim her as their own as do the people of Scotland where she was built.

"But Liverpool had to wait for 21 years to see the reality of the dream sail up the Mersey; and when QE2 anchored for the first time off The Pier Head in 1990 the wait seemed worthwhile.

"More than one million Merseysiders lined both banks of the river to give her the greatest welcome she has ever had. From that day forward QE2 kept faith with Liverpool; since then she has called here eight times.

"But the day which had to come some day has come today. Because this time, the ninth time, is the last time. She will not pass this way again."

Scenes from the Commemorative Concert at Liverpool Cathedral. The Band of the Welsh Guards, pictured right, were among those performing under the direction of Anthony Inglis

QE2: TIME TO SAY GOODBYE

COMMEMORATIVE CONCERT
AT LIVERPOOL CATHEDRAL
FRIDAY 3 OCTOBER 2008

THE MOST FAMOUS OCEAN LINERS IN THE WORLD™

THE LEAVING OF LIVERPOOL

DINNER ON BOARD
QUEEN ELIZABETH 2
FRIDAY 3 OCTOBER 2008

THE MOST FAMOUS OCEAN LINERS IN THE WORLD™

'I really loved that ship'

Captain Ian McNaught, Master of Queen Elizabeth 2, recalls the farewell round-Britain voyage and the call at Liverpool.

"That really was a special voyage, people were there to celebrate this wonderful ship and all that she stood for, and to visit rivers such as the Clyde and the Mersey, where the links were very strong, really brought the best of celebrations.

"Even after all her years of service I was always amazed by the numbers who were there to greet us and see us off, it was as if they were saying goodbye to their ship, a ship they had grown up with, and were now saying goodbye to. An old friend who had served them well.

"The Cathedral service in that call was very special, to be there sharing such an occasion with crew members and passengers was a great honour for me and my wife, to see the Paying Off Pennant paraded up the aisle really brought home that this was the beginning of the end for her, and to have to stand and speak from the pulpit that day and say goodbye was probably one of the most difficult and moving things I have ever done.

"I never made it to the end of the reading I had in front of me, I was so overcome that I just could not read the last few lines, I really loved that ship and all that went with her."

Later, Captain McNaught was to reveal how emotional he felt ascending the pulpit and representing QE2 for the last time in Liverpool.

The Cathedral fell silent in the moments immediately after his address and as he made his way down from the pulpit – the enormity of his words once again reminding the assembled guests that they were playing a part in history.

Within seconds, the Band of the Welsh Guards struck up the concert finale – Close Of Day. By the time the concert-goers returned to the ship, the crowds of spectators who had turned out all day long, were swelled by office workers and others converging on the waterfront after work to witness QE2's final departure from Liverpool.

After a spectacular fireworks display, accompanied by a Beatles tribute band performing at the Funnel bar on the ship's Sun Deck, QE2 let go her ropes for the last time in Liverpool. As she edged away from her berth at Princes Parade, tens of thousands of well-wishers cheered and waved to guests lining the open decks.

Soon she was gone.

2009

QUEEN MARY 2, TUESDAY, 20 OCTOBER

"There could be no prouder moment than to bring a great Cunarder home to Liverpool."

Commodore Bernard Warner,
Master, Queen Mary 2

During a distinguished sea carrier spanning more than 40 years, Cunard Commodore Bernard Warner had never taken a ship to Liverpool.

The gap in his CV was to be filled in the most spectacular way possible when it was announced that Queen Mary 2 would make her maiden call at Liverpool on 20 October, 2009.

Britain's flagship was celebrating her fifth year in service with a lap of honour around the British Isles, taking in an historic call at Greenock on the Clyde, where 125 ships had been built for Cunard, before heading south towards the Mersey where she became, and remains, the largest passenger liner ever to sail up the river to the city's famous Pier Head waterfront.

For Commodore Warner, the prospect of writing another chapter in the history of Cunard and Liverpool promised to provide unforgettable memories.

"I had a feeling of great pride on hearing that Queen Mary 2 was to call at Liverpool on her circumnavigation of the British Isles in 2009," recalls the retired Commodore.

"Liverpool is steeped in Cunard history, the spiritual home, and the port from which Samuel Cunard himself sailed on his first ship in 1840. As we prepared for the maiden call to the Mersey by Queen Mary 2, I found myself pondering who, in 1840, could possibly imagine the size of ship that would emerge from such small beginnings."

The paddle steamer Britannia, which was to revolutionise transatlantic passenger travel, could be accommodated inside the main restaurant bearing her name on Queen Mary 2.

Commodore Warner recalls an air of excitement and anticipation on board the liner as she made her way round the British coast.

"Liverpool was to be the highlight – the call at the spiritual home, but after leaving Southampton, as we headed north, preparations were made with the Royal National Lifeboat Institution (RNLI) to sail close to Whitby harbour on the North East coast of Yorkshire, to honour a recently deceased lifeboat man.

"Whitby has a strong personal attachment for me. It was where my love of the sea had been nurtured during summer holidays with my parents in the 1950s.

"So, whereas Whitby had provided a strong personal attachment for me, Liverpool was the ancestral home of Cunard and held emotional ties with Queen Mary 2 and all her ship's company.

"Having called at South Queensferry, Edinburgh, on 17 October, dropping anchor close to the Forth Railway Bridge, we arrived in Greenock on Monday, 19 October. It was here that our Mersey pilot boarded so that final preparations for our arrival at Liverpool could be made with the Bridge team, and so lay the platform for a seamless arrival into the Mersey the following morning," recalls the Commodore.

On 95% of her dockings around the world, Queen Mary 2 can berth under her own power. "However," the Commodore remembers, "owing to the strength of tide and after much discussion with the pilots we decided to order three tugs on this occasion."

An additional challenge for the Bridge team that day was coping with a five to six-knot flood tide running on arrival at the Liverpool Landing Stage.

Commodore Warner takes up the account of the morning's events: "We crossed the Mersey Bar with ample water beneath the ship. With a draft of over 10 metres, we were not only the largest liner to enter the port of Liverpool, but we also had a deeper draft than all our predecessors.

"As had been predicted, the flood tide was running with the ship at up to six knots, and the plan was to turn the ship around in ample time, before stemming the tide and taking her alongside the Landing Stage starboard side to.

"Whenever possible, and regardless of the size or manoeuvrability of their ship, most seafarers like to stem the current to dock their ship. This offers more flexibility and ease of control, thus making any operation of this nature that much safer.

"With the tugs in assistance we started to swing the ship just off Wallasey Town Hall, which was the best part of a mile upstream from our berth. As she made her turn, Queen Mary 2 was allowed to drift along with the tide ever further up the Mersey, until such time as she was pointing towards the berth. Ahead power was then used to delicately ease the ship alongside, using the strong tide on the bow to assist the ship onto the floating landing stage.

Commodore Bernard Warner, the Master of Queen Mary 2, helps passengers disembark at the Liverpool Cruise Terminal.

"Queen Mary 2 does not have conventional rudders, but is steered by two azimuthing propellers. There are four large propellers at the stern of the ship, each approximately six metres in diameter, and each propeller is attached to the forward end of a pod, which contains the electric drive motor. Two of these giant pods can rotate through 360 degrees, and the two forward props are fixed and just give ahead or astern movement. This configuration gives extreme manoeuvrability at the stern of the ship.

"Another interesting fact about the propellers is that they pull the liner through the water and do not push as on most conventional ships," explains Commodore Warner. "Each of these pods with the prop attached weighs the equivalent of a laden Boeing 747.

"At the bow, there are three thrusters mounted in tunnels running beneath the waterline. These draw water in from one side of the ship and throw it out on the other, thus creating the thrust to move the bow in synchronization with the stern.

"As the ship drew alongside the berth and was making her lines fast, I became aware of the thousands of people who had come out to welcome us on Queen Mary 2's maiden call at Liverpool.

"Having been at sea for over 40 years, this was my first call at Liverpool in any ship, igniting a memory that will live in my thoughts always. There could be no prouder moment than to bring a great Cunarder home to Liverpool."

Safe alongside by 1145hrs, it soon became apparent to those on board that this was going to be a very special day.

Crowds thronged the Liverpool waterfront.

Private and pleasure craft on the river observed the ship's security zone, their skippers edging as close as they were permitted to the great liner. The Mersey Ferry Royal Daffodil continued its run of sightseeing cruises, each one fully booked.

Overhead, media helicopters, flying to record the dramatic arrival, dispersed and returned to their bases allowing memorable and dramatic footage to hit the lunchtime news bulletins.

Taking their place, and keeping the story running, a posse of reporters and cameramen waited patiently at the foot of Queen Mary 2's gangway. The wait was worth their while as Commodore Warner disembarked the ship with Cunard's then President, Peter Shanks.

"There was a frenzy of TV and other media interviews," he recalls. Liverpool were playing in the Champions League at Anfield that night against Lyon and the Sports News crews came down as well. It was a reminder of the level of interest Queen Mary 2 generates."

The Commodore told reporters: "It is absolutely amazing to bring such a big ship – the largest ocean liner in the world – into Liverpool, and indeed the largest passenger ship ever to

Thousands of people turned up to welcome Queen Mary 2 for her maiden call to Liverpool, with many national flags on display

come up the Mersey. So it is a very proud moment for me but, more particularly, we have some very excited guests who are thrilled to be here in Liverpool today and people were all out on the dockside to wave and cheer us as we came in and we were blowing the whistles as well and that got them excited!"

Civic functions followed on board and included a plaque exchange between the ship and the City of Liverpool. At these, the limelight was taken by a young girl who approached the Commodore and announced that she shared her birthday (8 January, 2004) with Queen Mary 2 and presented a birthday card for the ship. "We were speechless," recalls Peter Shanks. "We sent for Cunard teddy bears in return!"

A concert was to take place on board in the ship's vast Royal Court Theatre.

Some 63 Hallé Orchestra musicians were joined by soprano Helen Williams and tenor Jon Christos under the musical direction of Anthony Inglis, returning to Queen Mary 2 five years after directing musicians and soloists at the ship's stunning naming ceremony.

Throughout the evening, thousands of spectators descended on the waterfront. On the opposite side of the Mersey, vantage points also became thronged with people taking in the dramatic sight of the largest ocean liner in the world at Pier Head.

If her arrival that morning had been impressive, her departure was to be dramatic with a spectacular firework display illuminating the huge ship as well as the Three Graces.

As the final fireworks faded, orders were given for Queen Mary 2 to let go her ropes and engage her sophisticated propulsion system to edge away from the berth.

For those on board it was a tumultuous sail away from Cunard's spiritual home.

For those still packing every vantage point along both sides of the river, and aboard special Mersey Ferry farewell cruises, it was the highlight of a most memorable day for Liverpool and Cunard.

Two Liverpool FC fans on board Queen Mary 2 proudly show off their banner as the ship berths in the city, with many people keen to capture the historic event on camera

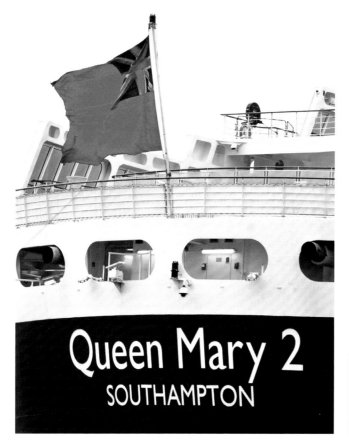

2010

QUEEN VICTORIA, MONDAY, 26 JULY

"The welcome was terrific. We saw the public from a long way away. There were a lot of people out there to see us all day long."

Captain Paul Wright, Master, Queen Victoria

Nothing seems to diminish the public's appetite to turn out and see Cunard ships in the Mersey. Less than a year after the overwhelming success of Queen Mary 2's first call, and less than two years after the city bid its very fond farewell to the legendary Queen Elizabeth 2, preparations were being made for Liverpool to welcome Queen Victoria, the newest addition to the fleet.

Each successive call at Liverpool since QE2's first in 1990 had served to underline the links between the company and the city.

History and heritage play a powerful part in the Cunard marketing mix, and nowhere else in the world can lay claim to the role Liverpool has successfully played in the company's history.

For the city, with its much-vaunted and long-awaited cruise liner facility finally up and running, and emerging from its top billing, centre stage as European Capital of Culture in 2008, the impact of Cunard calls was not lost.

Civic and business leaders recognised the huge opportunity the cruise industry represented and the more savvy (and less arrogant) realised the world's cruise ships would not form an orderly queue at the Mersey Bar, waiting to visit Liverpool, unless the city actively and credibly marketed itself as a cruise destination.

The profile and success generated by each Cunard call were becoming a very valuable marketing tool for Liverpool.

Passengers on board Queen Victoria, in Liverpool for the first time, take in the surroundings while, left, the ship is viewed from West Tower

Her Royal Highness the Duchess of Cornwall meets passengers and crew members on board Queen Victoria and, below right, cuts the cake to celebrate the 170th anniversary of the first Cunard vessel to leave Liverpool

Stunning images of Queen Mary 2 turning in the Mersey in front of the Three Graces formed a dramatic backdrop to the city's stand at the annual, global cruise industry get-together in Miami.

Being able to demonstrate its capacity to handle the biggest ocean liner in the world, together with increasingly impressive guest feedback on the offer of the city and wider destination, was doing Liverpool no harm in the eyes of the industry moguls.

The maiden call by the newest Cunarder, scheduled for 26 July, 2010, was certain to attract further public as well as cruise trade interest.

When it was announced that Her Royal Highness the Duchess of Cornwall would visit the ship at Liverpool, the day became even more significant.

The Duchess, accompanied by her husband, His Royal Highness the Prince of Wales, had named Queen Victoria at a lavish ceremony in Southampton on 10 December, 2007,

and a portrait commemorating her association with the ship hangs in the Grand Lobby.

Performing these official duties at Southampton (during which the Christening bottle failed to break against the ship's bow), and throughout her guided tour of the liner, the Duchess took a very keen interest in the crew and their numerous roles and responsibilities on board as they prepared for Queen Victoria's maiden voyage.

With Cunard's support of the Prince's Trust and aware of the genuine interest the Duchess had in the ship and its crew, executives were keen to welcome the Duchess back on board at Liverpool.

The prospect of witnessing a Royal Visit, as well as a Cunard's newest liner in the Mersey, helped swell the crowds filling Pier Head and Princes Parade.

A fault on the helicopter bringing the Royal party north that morning meant the crowds had to be patient for their first glimpse of the Duchess.

Rain and low cloud over the waterfront did nothing to lighten the atmosphere but, eventually, about an hour later than scheduled the Royal Party arrived at the gangway and was welcomed on board.

Despite the delay in her schedule, the Duchess remained on board longer than had been anticipated, meeting crew members from various departments before a reception with invited passengers and other guests in the Queens Room.

Reflecting on the day's events, Queen Victoria's Master, Captain Paul Wright, said afterwards: "I am sorry we have not been here before!

"We have been out two-and-a-half years but we leave the best till last!

"The welcome was terrific. We saw the public from a long way away. There were a lot of people out there to see us. We had two Mersey Ferries come out even in the rain and the mist they came out and they were full and it was fantastic to see them.

"We were honoured too to welcome back Her Royal Highness the Duchess of Cornwall to visit Queen Victoria. It has been a great and memorable day for all of our guests."

Left, Queen Victoria's Master, Captain Paul Wright, waves to the crowds after the ship arrives in Liverpool

2011

QUEEN ELIZABETH, THURSDAY, 8 SEPTEMBER
QUEEN MARY 2, THURSDAY, 15 SEPTEMBER

"It is a very special occasion today. We take this ship around the world but this is our maiden call now to our spiritual home of Liverpool. Thank you for being here to welcome us."

Captain Christopher Wells, Master, Queen Elizabeth

Maiden calls at Liverpool were becoming a rite of passage for new Cunarders, their Captains and their crews.

While Captain Paul Wright had waited two-and-a-half years for the opportunity to introduce Queen Victoria to its owners' spiritual home, his colleague Captain Chris Wells was able to sail up the Mersey less than one year after his ship, Queen Elizabeth, had been named in Southampton by Her Majesty Queen Elizabeth II on 11 October, 2010.

When she entered service, the new Queen Elizabeth gave Cunard the youngest ocean fleet in the world.

Her call at Liverpool on 8 September, 2011, came during a British Isles cruise taking in Edinburgh (South Queensferry), Inverness and Glasgow (Greenock) before Liverpool.

It promised to be both another important opportunity for Liverpool as well as a busy day on the waterfront.

The visit also marked the start of a week when Cunard's commitment to the city was to be underlined by the return to the Mersey of Queen Mary 2, scheduled to make her second call at Pier Head on 15 September.

Before that, preparations to welcome her new little sister were being finalised.

Queen Elizabeth shares the same hull design and classification as her sister Queen Victoria. Both were designed and built by the same Italian shipbuilding and engineering company, Fincantieri, and their interior layouts are very similar.

Externally, the liners differ at the stern and on the upper decks where additional facilities and deck space have been added on Queen Elizabeth, points and details not lost on the small army of ship-spotters and enthusiasts gathered along both sides of the Mersey awaiting her arrival.

The highlight of the maiden call was the third in the series of unique concerts arranged by Cunard and staged at Liverpool Cathedral.

During her visits to the city in 2007 and 2008, Queen Elizabeth 2's guests had enjoyed these milestone events in Cunard's history.

To mark the first arrival at Liverpool of the new ship, the specially created and arranged Commemorative Concert programme was called "The Magnificent Elizabeths".

It was to follow the successful model of the earlier events and feature a range of pieces and performances from the Royal Liverpool Philharmonic Orchestra, the Liverpool Cathedral Choir, the Liverpool Welsh Choral, the Band of the Welsh Guards, Organist Professor Ian Tracey and

sopranos Lesley Garrett and Jenny Williams, all under the direction once again of Anthony Inglis.

Each piece of music was interspersed with short speeches made by a variety of people associated with The Magnificent Elizabeths – the final line of their address marking the cue for the next piece of music.

These included Florence "Dennie" Farmer, Madrina to Queen Elizabeth. Her husband Willie joined Cunard in 1938 and went on to complete 41 years of service, including the position of Chief Engineer on the Queen Elizabeth and the Queen Elizabeth 2.

She told the Concert guests: "I was brought up in the Midlands, and the sea was something I saw once a year at Skegness. But as a young woman I was taken to Southampton

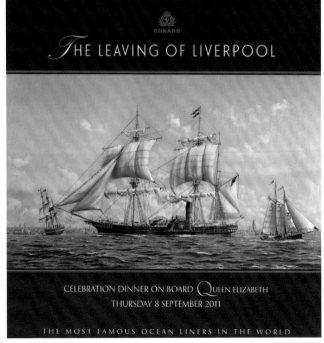

THE LEAVING OF LIVERPOOL

CELEBRATION DINNER ON BOARD QUEEN ELIZABETH
THURSDAY 8 SEPTEMBER 2011

THE MOST FAMOUS OCEAN LINERS IN THE WORLD

to look at the ships. I was totally unprepared for the size of Queen Elizabeth, whose two funnels dominated the skyline. I was overawed by it. We were taken on a guided tour of the public rooms, and I recall touching the wood panels to make sure they were real. I was fascinated by the white tablecloths and sparkling silver and china. It was much grander than the Lyons Corner House I was used to.

"Little did I imagine then that my future husband would one day become Chief Engineer on Queen Elizabeth. He joined the ship on her very first sailing in 1940 – a secret dash, the ship still unfinished, from the yard on the Clyde to New York. He'd been told to pack a bag for the weekend – but the weekend turned into three years as Queen Elizabeth, along with Queen Mary and Aquitania, began to carry troops to

Queen Elizabeth makes her way up the River Mersey while, above right, Florence 'Dennie' Farmer is pictured after welding coins of good luck to the mast of the ship after becoming its Madrina and, right, the Commemorative Dinner Menu for Liverpool

The original Queen Elizabeth, pictured in 1948, three years after the end of the Second World War. Opposite, the current Queen Elizabeth makes her way towards Fort Perch Rock lighthouse

Europe and the Far East from Australia and New Zealand.

"Later, in tandem with Queen Mary, she brought American GIs to Europe – 15,000 at a time, unescorted and at full speed across the Atlantic. Hitler offered a reward to any U Boat commander who could sink either of the Queens - but they were faster not only than the U Boats, but also faster than the torpedoes. Sir Winston Churchill acknowledged that in carrying out their phenomenal trooping duties, the Queens considerably shortened the war.

"It was a sad day when my husband Bill and I saw film of Queen Elizabeth burning in Hong Kong harbour years later. When Queen Mary 2 went to Hong Kong for the first time, Commodore Warner invited me to the Bridge. It was dusk, and light was fading as we passed over the grave of this once mighty ship. I was asked to ring 8 bells on the Queen

Elizabeth bell. It was a very poignant moment and brought home to me just how much Queen Elizabeth meant not just to me, but to the people of Britain. She was a symbol of all we hold dear, she had a fighting spirit and she defended our island to the end."

As Mrs Farmer descended from the pulpit, the Orchestra and Choirs performed a special arrangement of Parry's England.

Next to speak was former Cunard Social Hostess and Madrina to Queen Victoria, Maureen Ryan.

Addressing the 2,000 guests, she said: "I first sailed on Queen Elizabeth in 1964 as Lady Assistant Purser – or Lady Ape in the terminology of the excruciatingly witty young male Assistant Pursers.

"And even though Queen Elizabeth was coming to the

end of her reign, she was still hugely glamorous – an art deco masterpiece that, even so late in her life, beautifully captured the post war golden era of transatlantic travel. Her role was rapidly being taken over by the jet aeroplanes but no aeroplane could match the glamour of Queen Elizabeth.

"I well recall doing safe deposit duty in the evenings, when beautifully dressed and coiffured ladies, accompanied by elegant men in evening dress, took the family jewels from their deposit boxes to dine and dance in the legendary Verandah Grill. Among them might be Elizabeth Taylor, and Dirk Bogarde was a regular passenger.

"It was such fun for a young girl – especially when you received a whispered message 'the train leaves at midnight'. It was code to go to the forward B Staircase at midnight, and take the lift down to the Coffin Club, the most discreet and unusual nightspot in the world. It was run by Stan, resplendent in a dinner jacket, who was keeper of the coffins and spare lifejackets in the bowels of Queen Elizabeth. As the ship thundered through the black North Atlantic night, we – officers, passengers and crew – surrounded by these objects of survival and disposal, really did dance all night."

Accompanied by the Royal Liverpool Philharmonic Orchestra, soprano Lesley Garrett sang I Could Have Danced All Night.

A former member of the Purser's team on Queen Elizabeth, Keith Gledhill, told the hushed Cathedral: "I was just a sheltered 18-year-old from Blackpool when I first joined Queen Elizabeth.

"What a different world it was from the one I had known! We had just come through the war, and years of rationing had made the world seem grey and austere. But on Queen Elizabeth, with no rationing and glamorous passengers at every turn, my grey world suddenly went Technicolor.

"I remember the excitement I felt in the First Class Purser's Office seeing people I'd only ever seen on the screen at the Saturday morning pictures back in Blackpool. And when, on my very first morning I had to deal with the legendary Bette Davis – accompanied on this occasion by her husband rather than Baby Jane – I thought I was in the movies myself.

"It was a magical world for a young man, and as we shuttled back and forth from Southampton to New York at 30 knots with fabulous food, famous people, millionaires and Royalty, it seemed like one long carnival.

"But carnivals end; and this began to wind down in 1968

when Cunard sold Queen Elizabeth just a year after selling her sister Queen Mary. And then, in January 1971, under her new owners, Queen Elizabeth caught fire and sank in Hong Kong Harbour. All I have now to remind me of her is a beautiful brass pen made from the metal of one of the salvaged portholes. The carnival really was over."

Soprano Jenny Williams, accompanied by the orchestra, then sang The Carnival Is Over.

The focus of the special programme then turned to Queen Elizabeth 2

Actress Anna Bentinck turned to speak.

She told those present: "Though I'm not sure how much we realised it at the time the sixties are looked upon now as an age of excitement and innovation, of breaking free from the old ways – a kind of great leap forward.

"It was the age of the mini-skirt and the Mini, Concorde and the man on the moon, Twiggy, Mary Quant, the Beatles and the Rolling Stones.

"But it was also the age of QE2 – a ship that struggled to be born at a time of industrial strife and the decline of passenger shipping, but which, like a butterfly, opened her wings to become one of the great style icons of the age.

"I was an aspiring actress at the time, still at school. And when the opportunity arose to appear in a film about the construction and introduction of QE2, I leapt at it – attending the audition in my school uniform.

"The male part in the film was a choice between two young men – and I was allowed to choose. I picked the bouncy, floppy-haired blue-eyed Murray Head; I rejected the rather odd hunched and somewhat miserable one. I learned later he was called David Bowie.

"Filming included the Maiden Voyage to New York, and among our companions were Ringo Starr and George Harrison; they didn't like flying and loved the ship.

"And QE2 was welcomed in New York for the first time in a manner to which she became accustomed all over the world in later years – with fireworks, flotillas and an official welcome by Mayor John Lindsay.

"She was a leader in an age where Britain led the world – the age of Aquarius."

Liverpool hosted two Cunard calls within a week in 2011 with Queen Mary 2 following Queen Elizabeth

For this rousing, change of pace, Jenny Williams was accompanied by the Band of the Welsh Guards in a performance which resonated all around the Cathedral's great space.

As the Concert drew towards its close, Coronation Street actor Roy Barraclough walked towards the pulpit and prepared to address the guests in front of him.

He said: "When I was young, Britannia really did rule the waves. This country had one of the biggest naval fleets in the world, one of the biggest merchant fleets in the world, and one of the biggest shipbuilding industries in the world.

"Well, it's not quite the same now, is it?

"But one way in which we do still rule the waves is in tradition and in standards at sea. I've been sailing with Cunard now for many years, as have most of you, and I have yet to be disappointed. Whether it was Queen Elizabeth 2, Queen Mary 2 or Queen Victoria, the sense of occasion, the standards of food and service, and the faint whiff of seafaring tradition have combined into perfection. There is always the risk that tradition can fossilise but, as the current Cunard fleet demonstrates, it is perfectly possible to innovate and be traditional — and contrive to take your loyal passengers with you.

"Unlike most of you, I haven't sailed on Queen Elizabeth

yet, and I'm looking forward to doing that later this year; I just know she is going to be every bit as good as my current favourite, Queen Victoria. I know that because Cunard is so successful at carrying the best of the past into the future.

"So let's celebrate Queen Elizabeth's maiden arrival in Cunard's home city of Liverpool; let's celebrate the fact that the best of Cunard traditions, which started here, go on. At the same time let's celebrate the ditching of some less successful traditions. When Charles Dickens left from this port for Boston one hundred and seventy years ago on Cunard's Britannia, he lamented the fact that his cabin was a 'profoundly preposterous box', that the passengers' saloon was 'a hearse with windows', that his pillow was 'like a muffin beaten flat'. Or that his mattress was 'a sticking plaster attached to a shelf'. Those traditions, along with the carrying of a cow on deck to provide fresh milk, have thankfully gone. What we are left with, is simply the best.

"Let's celebrate the fact that, in some ways at least, Britannia does still rule the waves."

Lesley Garrett returned to the microphone and with the Philharmonic Orchestra, and audience singing each chorus, delivered a spell-binding performance.

As the huge cathedral once again fell silent, the Master of Queen Elizabeth, Captain Christopher Wells, walked to the microphone.

"Cunard has come a long way since our very first ship left Liverpool, bound for Halifax and Boston, in July 1840," he told the audience.

"We were pioneers, establishing the first ever scheduled steamship service across the Atlantic. But we were also rather basic, as Charles Dickens' comments referred to by Roy Barraclough attest.

"In those days the ships were tiny — Britannia, the first ship, would fit inside the Royal Court Theatre on Queen Elizabeth — and they were uncomfortable. Passengers were often ankle deep in water: "Officer, there's water pouring down the stairs" said one passenger to one of my predecessors. "We only worry, Madam", he replied, "when it's coming up the stairs." Sounds like one of the comments I'd get into trouble for. But by the time the first Elizabeth put to sea, exactly 100 years after our first ship set sail, how things had changed! Although the first Elizabeth entered service in the stripped down austerity of wartime, once she began civilian service in 1946 she blossomed.

"Along with Queen Mary, she became a beacon on excellence, a home-from-home for millionaires and magnates, stars and politicians, as well as for ordinary folk

crossing the Atlantic maybe as tourists or to see relations or to start a new life.

"Each ship, like the company as a whole, was a family – a family entire of itself, largely cut off from the world for the length of a transatlantic crossing.

"Probably no family was closer than the QE2's family – never has a ship had so many dedicated fans, who travelled in her again and again, each time reacquainting themselves not just with officers and crew but with fellow passengers first encountered on earlier voyages.

"Our new Queen Elizabeth is set to follow that pattern. Already, though she is not even a year old, she is gathering a family – people who have travelled on her more than once in her eleven brief months of life.

"Cunard, one of the oldest names in shipping, now has the youngest fleet at sea. The future hasn't looked better since – well, since 1840.

"But whatever new ships we introduce, the Cunard style will be evident on them all. And the Cunard family will be on board.

"To travel with Cunard, now or in 20 years' time, means you'll never walk alone."

Lesley Garrett, the Orchestra, Cathedral Choir and Welsh Choral combined to perform a very memorable version of the anthem adopted by Liverpool Football Club.

The crescendo marked a fitting finale to The Magnificent Elizabeths Commemorative Concert.

Less than a week later it was the turn of the flagship Queen Mary 2 to return to centre stage on the Mersey for her second call at Liverpool on 15 September, 2011.

"Liverpool and Cunard history are intrinsically linked and we will continue to celebrate that link."

Angie Redhead,
Operations Manager, Cruise Liverpool

2012

QUEEN ELIZABETH, FRIDAY, 3 AUGUST

Members of the Liverpool Ukulele Orchestra performed for passengers coming off Queen Elizabeth

The popularity of Cunard's Round Britain cruises was increasing each year, ensuring Liverpool's place in the itineraries and brochures.

Starting in Southampton, these voyages invariably take an easterly route along the English Channel to the North Sea where a day and night would be spent heading for South Queensferry on the Firth of Forth and with easy access to Edinburgh; a call at Inverness followed by Kirkwall in the Orkney Islands, Greenock on the Clyde and then Liverpool.

Onwards from the Mersey, the itinerary usually includes Dublin and Cobh in Ireland, a day at anchor in the Channel Islands followed by an overnight course back to Southampton.

Where schedules and planning permit, these itineraries often dovetail with an Eastbound Crossing of the Atlantic from New York to Southampton, with Queen Mary 2 arriving in port on the morning of the day one of her smaller sisters departs from an adjacent terminal for a lap of the British Isles. The opportunity to do both an Atlantic crossing and a tour of Britain holds strong appeal for many US guests.

In 2012, the Round Britain turn of duty fell to Queen Elizabeth and she made her second visit to Liverpool on Friday, 3 August.

Before arriving in Liverpool, much attention on board had been focussed on the London Olympics with the spectacular opening ceremony broadcast live on a large screen inside the ship's Royal Court Theatre, and live daily action shown on several large screens in the Golden Lion pub.

The call fell in the middle of the summer holidays and on

Cruise Liverpool Operations Manager Angie Redhead

a day of fine weather, ensuring large crowds of shore side spectators throughout the day and evening.

Among visitors invited on board were representatives of various departments within Liverpool City Council who would have a part to play in the staging of any major events to mark Cunard's 175th anniversary three years later, Cunard being keen to understand what the city could deliver as well as the practical aspects of accommodating the entire fleet together in the Mersey.

It would be another year before Cunard was able to announce its Three Queens spectacular for Liverpool.

Cruise Liverpool Operations Manager Angie Redhead is in no doubt about the importance and value of the relationship between Liverpool and Cunard.

"Since the official opening of the Cruise Terminal in 2007 with QE2, we have managed every year to host at least one Cunard ship and create some sort of 'show' – the photos that follow have become the backbone of our fantastic image gallery.

"To see a ship berthed just metres from our World Heritage Site says more about Liverpool Cruise Terminal than a brochure or a website could do. The impact is instant – it looks glorious; which cruise line wouldn't want their passengers to experience that?

"Liverpool and Cunard history are intrinsically linked and we will continue to celebrate that link whilst welcoming new cruise lines to create their own unique history with us.

"Cunard celebrations will be the 'flagship' events of 2015. Our intention is to celebrate Liverpool's maritime history, as the birthplace of the first passenger cruise line, in conjunction with Cunard's historic connections with Liverpool and its people.

"Both the Three Queens rendezvous in May and the commemorative sailing of Queen Mary 2 from Liverpool in July will bookend a city wide programme of events that will run throughout the summer of 2015 appealing to local, national and international audiences.

"The events we have in place will be visually spectacular, artistically adventurous, striking, engaging and of exceptional quality to really capture a memorable historic moment in time and encapsulate the character and passion of Liverpool.

"It is a once in a lifetime opportunity for Liverpool. The meeting of all three Cunard Queens has only taken place in a handful of locations across the world and we aim to make the most of that moment to the delight and wonder of both passengers and spectators."

2013

QUEEN MARY 2, FRIDAY, 17 MAY

QUEEN ELIZABETH, TUESDAY, 6 AUGUST

"The atmosphere on the watefront is
still very special and unique to Cunard calls."

Angie Redhead, Operations Manager, Cruise Liverpool

Liverpool secured its hat-trick of calls by Queen Mary 2 on 17 May, 2013 – the appearance of the huge liner in the Mersey once again attracting significant crowds to the waterfront.

The call was the first of two by Cunard that year with Queen Elizabeth scheduled alongside later in the summer, the company continuing to commit to the city and the development of its cruise business.

Itinerary planning is a complex process for cruise operators, whose operational teams have to juggle a whole host of variables in planning the deployment of their ships around the world.

These teams often work two or three years in advance of the sailings they plan so carefully.

At the time of these 2013 calls to Liverpool, Cunard's UK PR team had already been considering for some time where to deploy the Three Queens in 2015 – the year that would mark the 175th anniversary of Britannia's first departure from Liverpool back in 1840.

Liverpool was an obvious location to consider hosting some part of the 175 celebrations but there was absolutely no room for any complacency from the city.

Informal discussions between the parties had been going on sporadically for almost three years. Hearts and minds elsewhere still had to be won over to the idea that Liverpool should take centre stage in 2015 and, behind the scenes, a great deal of work had been done to establish if Liverpool could accommodate a gathering of the Three Queens.

Against this backdrop – and mindful of the timeline for key decisions about 2015 being made by Cunard – Liverpool was determined to put on another good show during each of the 2013 calls.

These efforts were rewarded on the afternoon of Tuesday, 12 November, 2013 when the Mayor of Liverpool received a telephone call from Cunard's communications team in Southampton confirming the news that Liverpool would indeed host a rendezvous of the Three Queens in 2015, and also that the original 1840 transatlantic voyage would be recreated in a sailing departing Liverpool 175 years to the day since Britannia left the Mersey for North America.

Before the phone call and public announcement in November, 2013, Liverpool did indeed put on another good show welcoming and hosting Queen Mary 2 and Queen Elizabeth.

Pivotal to the success of these – and every other cruise ship visit to Liverpool Cruise Terminal – is the team led by Cruise & Operations Manager Angie Redhead.

By the end of 2014, Angie and her team had managed a total of 175 cruise ship operations since Queen Elizabeth 2 arrived to open the berth in 2007.

One of her most memorable events surrounds the arrival of Her Royal Highness the Duchess of Cornwall during Queen Elizabeth's call in 2010.

"Any Royal visit requires a lot of co-ordination and planning well in advance of the actual event, down to the tiniest detail. When Camilla visited in 2010, security was at an extremely high level and we had a number of close protection officers on site.

"Our plan had been tested numerous times in fine detail and as the Incident Manager for the cruise terminal, I was to be the liaison between cruise personnel and police should anything untoward occur. For this reason, I advised my team that until Camilla was safely on board the ship, they were not to contact me via radio or speak with me about any general cruise operations – this was all to be delegated to my Deputy, Jack Leyland.

"I took the call from the Police driver that they were just five minutes away in the car and I alerted the team at which point one of them asked me in a panicky, urgent voice if I was meeting Camilla and if so would I like him to remove

the seagull 'present' from my shoulder....We still laugh about this seagull incident now. In seven years of working on site I have never been targeted before or since; what are the chances!"

Angie and her team are well placed to gauge the unique impact a Cunard call makes on the city.

"There is definitely a resonance with Cunard ships calling into Liverpool, more so than any other cruise line," she says.

"I believe this is due to the history shared between the city and the cruise line during an era when Liverpool was a major passenger shipping hub. Everyone in Liverpool it seemed, had a family member who went to sea and who more often than not worked on Cunard ships. Their stories have been shared with children and grandchildren so when a Cunard ship calls in, it becomes something of a family occasion.

"Over the years, we as a city have identified that huge numbers of people from all over the northwest make their way to the Pier Head to see these Cunard ship visits and so we now use this as an opportunity to showcase Liverpool to a wider audience.

Celebrity hairdresser Herbert Howe waves goodbye to his sisters, Pat McCrystal, Trica Davies and Christine Lawton, who were embarking Queen Elizabeth

"There is an anticipation and expectation that there will be music, street theatre, fireworks and so on, but I have to say even without all of those things, the atmosphere is still very special and unique to Cunard calls."

She believes each Cunard call represents a huge opportunity for the city.

"Cunard calls are a showcase for the city. It shows the world that we are a city that values its maritime history but is also forging a new future as a major player in the modern day cruise industry.

"The sense of occasion is tangible whether you are here at the waterfront or watching on the news or are simply looking at the aerial photographs that follow showing these wonderful ships at our magnificent waterfront with thousands of people all around.

"It sends the message to the global cruise industry that cruise business matters to us as a city and as a population."

2014

QUEEN VICTORIA, FRIDAY, 30 MAY
AND SATURDAY, 31 MAY

"Thank you Liverpool!
You did us proud!"

*Commodore Christopher Rynd,
Master, Queen Victoria*

Queen Victoria's second call at Liverpool at the end of May 2014 proved to be one of the most memorable Cunard events in the city since July 1990.

It came just one week short of a year away from the Three Queens spectacular for which detailed planning was now underway.

It also staked its own place in history by being the first overnight call by a Cunard ship to the Mersey for almost 50 years, and by being on the exact 100th anniversary of the maiden voyage departure from Liverpool of the revered Cunarder Aquitania.

Aquitania eventually came to be known as the "granny" of the Cunard line with 36 years' service.

She was one of the few big ships which saw service through both world wars, being converted into a troop ship in 1915 and carrying 30,000 men to the Dardanelles.

Winston Churchill credited her and the two Cunard Queens – Mary and Elizabeth – with shortening the Second World War by a year.

By the time she went for scrap in February 1950 she had steamed nearly three million miles and carried more than one million passengers. She was considered one of the most attractive ships of her time and one of the most beautiful four-funnelled liners.

The Aquitania's service length and miles sailed were both only surpassed by Queen Elizabeth 2.

Thus there was plenty to celebrate as Commodore Christopher Rynd brought Queen Victoria across the Mersey Bar on the morning of Friday, 30 May.

Since the last call at Liverpool, Cunard had confirmed its intention to stage the highlight of its 2015 celebrations in the spiritual home, setting up the prospect of one of the most memorable days in the city's history, as well as delighting civic leaders with its advertising strapline Three Queens, One Magnificent City.

There was further delight for them on board Queen Victoria that Friday evening when a huge exhibition stand bearing an image of the Three Queens beneath the headline: Liverpool 2015. The Fleet Is Coming was presented to Mayor Joe Anderson by Commodore Rynd and Carnival UK Chief Commercial Officer Gerard Tempest.

The presentation took place during a reception before a special dinner to commemorate the Aquitania anniversary.

Important though this date in Cunard and Liverpool's shared history undoubtedly is, there was no mistaking the topic of conversation on each table in the Verandah Restaurant that evening – The Three Queens Liverpool spectacular.

As well as the VIP civic guests, Cunard had also invited representatives form a number of Liverpool businesses and organisations it knew would be critical in the successful delivery of the 175th anniversary events.

Commodore Christopher Rynd salutes Jay St John as Queen Victoria docks in Liverpool

After their dinner, guests were escorted to the boat deck to take up prime vantage points for a stunning firework display launched from a barge in the Mersey.

Whilst they enjoyed an uninterrupted view of the pyrotechnics from the port side of the ship, they had no idea until the time came for them to disembark from the starboard side, what huge crowds had descended on the waterfront to view Queen Victoria and witness the spectacular celebrations.

The size of the turnout was not lost on the Cunard hosts or their guests. "If this is the turnout for one ship, imagine what it will be like when all three are here," said one.

Crowds remained on the waterfront until the early hours, taking advantage of clear skies in the late spring eventing to soak up what was a very special atmosphere at the Pier Head

as the Cunarder remained alongside overnight.

Saturday dawned bright and sunny. Commodore Rynd, accompanied by his wife, set off on specially arranged visits to Liverpool Cathedral and the Cunard Building.

As they returned to the cruise berth they were shown copies of the day's Liverpool Echo. The entire front page was devoted to a picture of the ship illuminated by the previous night's fireworks under the headline: Victorious!

As the morning ticked by, more and more spectators arrived on the waterfront, prompting many of the ship's passengers visiting Liverpool for the first time to pass positive comment about the location of the cruise berth and its proximity to the city's stunning waterfront.

Queen Victoria was due to leave, bound for Dublin, shortly before 1700hrs.

By the time final preparations were being made for the sail away, more than 20,000 people were gathered at the Pier Head and along the promenade next to the cruise berth. On the opposite side of the river, tens of thousands more were out to witness a ship sail down a river.

Anyone who doubts the pulling power of a Cunarder in the Mersey would do well to look at the wealth of images and film footage posted to social media sites through that day.

The impact of the visit was not lost on Cruise Liverpool's Operations Manager Angie Redhead.

"A combination of perfect weather with a Saturday afternoon departure resulted in what felt like the whole of Liverpool turning up to Pier Head to wave her off," recalls Angie.

"The city's Mezzo Soprano Danielle Thomas is a great friend of Cruise Liverpool and so we had asked her if she'd like to perform on departure of the ship with a few appropriate songs to mark such an occasion.

Making the headlines: How the Liverpool Echo reported
Queen Victoria's celebratory visit

"She opened with God Save The Queen which just set the tone for the rest of her performance of Rule Britannia, Land of Hope and Glory and You'll Never Walk Alone.

"Passengers were waving Union Jack flags and spectators were waving handkerchiefs and singing along.

"My relatively new cruise team had worked so hard during the overnight call of QV and had really stepped up and delivered so I called them all out onto the quayside, lined them up and told them to take a bow towards the ship.

"All of the passengers just burst into applause and cheers and whistles for the team most of whom were just overwhelmed and in tears by this point….they are security guards first and foremost and this was the first time they had ever had such recognition for doing their job.

"The atmosphere was amazing, a moment that's difficult to explain unless you were there but apparently, this departure was the talk of the ship for the rest of the voyage."

MAURETANIA
TRUE MONARCHS OF THE SEA

As well as the triumphant calls by the latter-day Cunard Queens, the Mersey has hosted other notable events involving giant Cunarders

On 11 July, 1913, HM King George V and HM Queen Mary accompanied by HRH Prince Edward, boarded the Mauretania in the Mersey.

The Royal party was conveyed to the giant liner by Mersey Docks and Harbour Board tender Galatea. The first Mauretania, sister to the ill-fated Lusitania, was a true Monarch of the Sea, designed to provide lavish public spaces on an unprecedented scale.

In the following year after the Royal Visit in Liverpool, Mauretania was called up for service in the First World War, serving as a speedy troop ship able to outrun enemy U boats. She was retired after distinguished service in 1935.

A little over three years later, on 28 July, 1938 the new, 35,738-ton Mauretania was launched from the slipway at Cammell Laird's world-famous Birkenhead shipbuilding yard. The formalities were performed by Lady Bates, wife of Cunard's Chairman Sir Percy Bates.

He and his Board Members had been able to follow the progress of the huge ship's construction from their offices in the Cunard Building opposite Laird's shipyard. There, the massive project had required the creation of huge timber scaffolds to allow the legions of yard workers access to the giant they were creating on Slipway Number 6 – previously occupied by the famous aircraft carrier Ark Royal.

As construction progressed, the second, two-funnelled Mauretania towered over the shipyard and surrounding areas of Birkenhead. At the time, she was the largest ship ever to be built in an English shipyard, and described as "a

floating repository of 20th century wonders". Mauretania sailed from Liverpool on her maiden voyage to New York on 17 June, 1939. Thousands of spectators crowded to vantage points on both sides of the river to give her and her guests – including many famous names – a send-off to remember. Overhead, aircraft dipped in salute and on the water, scores of craft escorted her on her way. At Liverpool Parish Church, a special peal of bells rang out across Pier Head. The great liner soon undertook wart service as a troopship for more than six years. Her first post-war Atlantic crossing from Liverpool to New York was in April 1947 and soon afterwards she was based in Southampton. The liner left Liverpool for the last time on 21 May, 1947. The second Mauretania was retired in 1965 and was eventually broken up in Scotland.

The Royal visit to Liverpool, above, and opposite, the first Mauretania leaves the River Tyne for her first trials at sea in 1907

These images show construction work taking place on the second Mauretania, a brochure for which can be seen on the opposite page. The view above was taken from a travelling crane at the bow and shows three of the lower decks in the course of construction at Cammell Laird's shipyard

Clockwise from far left: The launch of Mauretania, at the Cammell Laird yard in Birkenhead on 28 July, 1938; arriving in Southampton after her final voyage in 1965; at King George V Dock on the River Thames in 1939, where a large crowd can also be seen, and Captain John Treasure Jones at the controls in 1965

The triumph of a great tradition... Cunard's 2015 fleet – the three biggest Cunarders ever built

FIT FOR A
QUEEN

Cunard pioneered ocean travel 175 years ago. Today, the Fleet comprises the three biggest Cunarders ever built

As the sun rose over Manhattan on the morning of 25 April, 2004, some residents of the city that never sleeps were stopped in their tracks around Battery Park and on the banks of the Hudson River.

Their pause was momentary, a fleeting recognition that the place where they were was once again making and witnessing history: Queen Mary 2 and Queen Elizabeth 2 were meeting for the first time.

Not since March 1940 had two Cunard Queens been berthed in the port.

Now, 64 years on, as QE2 edged towards the point in the Hudson where she would swing starboard to make the 90-degree right turn to her berth on the south side of Pier 90, a new era of transatlantic liner travel was about to start.

Three days earlier, the new Cunard flagship Queen Mary 2 had arrived on the Pier, her graceful, steeply curved bow towering over port buildings to cast a shadow above the traffic slowing to a crawl on the road outside the port gates.

The largest, longest, tallest, widest and most expensive passenger liner ever built had made her mark.

As the old and the new icons of the Cunard fleet came closer together, whistle blows were exchanged.

◆ ◆

QUEEN MARY 2

Commodore Ron Warwick later recalled looking down from the bridge wing of Queen Mary 2 as his former charge edged towards her berth.

"I used to think QE2 was big, but as I waved to Captain Ian McNaught below us and across the Pier on the wing of QE2, I realised the difference."

A decade later, happily retired and in Southampton to board Queen Mary 2 for a celebratory 10th anniversary Atlantic crossing, the Commodore was once again reminded of the scale of another former charge. "I'd forgotten how big she is," he said as he exchanged greetings with regular guests and former colleagues.

Around the world, more people marvel at the size and scale of Queen Mary 2 from the outside, than view and experience the astonishing inside.

If the outside is impressive, the inside is stunning.

The sheer size and scale of the hull and superstructure, designed by naval architect Stephen Payne, presented the ship's interior design team with enormous public room space in which to create a unique city at sea.

Guests invariably board via the Grand Lobby, the six-storey structure which features a dramatic staircase and exclusive works of art.

At the start of every voyage, guests boarding here are greeted by Cunard Bell Boys, Stewards and Stewardesses who escort the new arrivals to their cabins.

Each grade of cabin is paired with a sea-view restaurant with Grills for the higher categories and restaurants for the deluxe and standard grades.

The main Dining Room, the Britannia Restaurant, seats 1,347 passengers, and is one of the most remarkable rooms at sea, spanning the full width of the ship and nearly three storeys in height with tiered dining on two levels.

The Britannia Restaurant evokes memories of classic ocean liner restaurants with a sweeping central staircase, an overhead light well and classic columns. A vast tapestry of a past Cunard liner hangs as a centrepiece.

Decorated in gold, the 200-seat Queens Grill is for the use of passengers booked in the highest-grade cabins and suites and hosts one of the finest dining experiences it is possible to enjoy at sea.

These passengers also have the exclusive use of the Queens Grill Bar (conveniently located next to the Grill) and Queens Grill Terrace on deck, a popular if not generously scaled retreat from busier open decks.

The intimate 178-seat Princess Grill, decorated in silver, is for passengers in the Junior Suite cabins. The exclusivity afforded to Grills guests does not extend as far as sea views from their restaurants — both are on promenade deck 7 allowing sundry joggers, power walkers and others passing by to view the goings on in the Grills, should they wish to do so.

The naval architect who designed Queen Mary 2, Stephen Payne, bottom right, watches the ship afloat for the first time at the Chantiers de l'Atlantique ship yard in Saint-Nazaire, France, in 2003

Queen Mary 2 offers several alternative dining venues. The 156-seat Todd English Restaurant on Deck 8 offers innovative Mediterranean cuisine in a modern setting. The room has been designed with intimate alcoves and architectural detailing and overlooks the Pool Terrace allowing al fresco dining when the weather allows.

The informal, some may consider it very informal, 478-seat King's Court serves breakfast and lunch buffet-style. It's often crowded and the flow of guests helping themselves to all before them can get frantic. Decorated screens transform the area into different dining venues at night: La Piazza (Italian); Lotus (Asian) and a British Carvery.

For snacks, the Boardwalk Café offers fast food choices outdoors and even the Golden Lion pub offers traditional English pub food for lunch.

The Royal Court Theatre, with tiered seating for 1,094, is the liner's main entertainment location with full-scale, West End-style productions as well as featured entertainers on the bill.

Queen Mary 2's Queens Room is the largest ballroom at sea, hosting ballroom dancing, cocktail parties and afternoon tea served with exemplary Cunard White Star Service.

It features a dramatic high ceiling more than seven metres high, crystal chandeliers, sweeping ocean views on both sides of the ship and the largest dance floor at sea measuring 7.5m by 13m.

Illuminations acts as a cinema, auditorium, lecture hall and broadcast studio. The room also hosts the first Planetarium at sea featuring a huge dome which is lowered over the auditorium to provide a screen for star shows and other presentations.

ConneXions is a unique education centre featuring facilities for Cunard's Enrichment programmes spanning topics and lectures as diverse as IT, Seamanship and Navigation, Art and Wine Appreciation.

The Winter Garden acts as Queen Mary 2's 'quiet area' and is reminiscent of a grand conservatory with flowers in bloom all year long.

The ship offers a range of 14 bars and clubs suiting a wide variety of tastes and providing a range of atmospheres, including an up-market modern Wine Bar (Sir Samuel's), a nautically-themed cocktail bar (The Chart Room) and the Veuve Clicquot Champagne Bar. Outdoors are Terrace Bar and the Regatta Bar.

The Empire Casino features the latest machines, traditional tables and an accompanying bar while the 5,000 square-foot Mayfair Shops offer eight different stores including designer boutiques.

The G32 nightclub is named after the hull number given to the ship by the French shipyard where she was built. It is strategically situated overlooking the stern of the ship, away from passenger cabins.

The forward Commodore Club observation lounge offers sweeping views over the bow. Connected to this room are the Boardroom and Cigar Lounge.

The Library and Bookshop is the largest to be found at sea and an extremely popular venue offering 8,000 hardbacks, 500 paperbacks, 200 audio books and newspapers and magazines. Children's facilities on board feature the very latest equipment for children of all ages, a permanent staff and nursery nurses. Children have their own dedicated inside/ outside play area.

Cunard's unique history is recalled in the Maritime Quest,

a museum-quality tour that tells the story of the most famous name in shipping.

Health and fitness facilities are among the largest and most extensive ever to be featured on board a ship and covering 20,000 square feet on two decks. The Spa offers services previously only found in luxurious, elite spas ashore. Facilities services include massages and therapeutic bodywork, mud, aromatherapy, seaweed treatments, facials and masks, conditioning body scrubs and body cocoons. There is also a complete gymnasium, thalassotherapy pool, whirlpool, herbal sauna, Finnish sauna, reflexology basins and an aromatic steam room. Throughout the ship there is a £3 million art collection on display.

Renowned international artists were commissioned to produce over 300 works of art from the painted ceiling in the Winter Garden to the huge tapestry in the Britannia Restaurant and a monumental sculptural relief in the Grand Lobby.

Other than the large indoor pool in the Spa, there are four

swimming pools outside. One of these can be covered by a retractable sliding glass roof to become an additional indoor pool if required.

Towering over 200 feet above sea level are sports facilities including two state-of-the-art golf simulators, a half-size basketball court, putting green, quoits, shuffleboard, deck games, a giant chess board and a paddle tennis court. There are eight whirlpool tubs.

Another classic feature is the expansive Promenade Deck, recreating an area which always served an important social function aboard transatlantic liners. This deck allows a 360° passage around the ship.

One lap of this deck circuit is just over one third of a mile. This generous deck also accommodates a line of full-length wooden steamer chairs. The medical facility is one of the largest and most modern of its kind afloat.

Queen Mary 2 also offers a Currency Exchange Service, Dry Cleaning and Laundry services and a Florist. In short, a true city at sea.

How flagship liner came to life

As well as a triumphant feat of design and engineering, the construction and entry into service of Queen Mary 2 was a remarkable demonstration of skilful project leadership and delivery engaging individuals and organisations from around the world.

Behind each and every date and landmark on this timeline lies a complex collaboration and collective effort involving hundreds of individuals who were each committed to their part in the creation of a new Cunard flagship.

1998

8 June
'Project Queen Mary' announced just one week after Carnival Corporation completes its purchase of Cunard Line. Plans to undertake the design and development of a new class of transatlantic liner unveiled.

1999

8 November
Cunard announces that the general arrangement plans for the new liner are completed. 'Project Queen Mary' to be the largest passenger ship ever built.

2000

10 March
Letter of Intent signed with Chantiers de l'Atlantique shipyard at Saint-Nazaire in France for the £550 million Queen Mary 2.

6 November
Formal contract signed in Paris by Micky Arison (Chairman and CEO of Carnival Corporation) and Patrick Boissier (President ALSTOM Marine and Chairman and CEO of Chantiers de l'Atlantique). At the same time in London the interior design for Queen Mary 2 is unveiled. Queen Mary 2 will be the largest, longest, tallest, widest and most expensive passenger ship ever.

2001

January
'Patron's Preview' programme launched granting passengers who sail on board QE2 and Caronia in 2001 an exclusive month-long preview of Queen Mary 2's maiden season.

February
Tank tests of Queen Mary 2 model successfully completed.

November
Cunard announces Canyon Ranch will operate the Health Spa.

2002

16 January
Pamela Conover, Cunard's President and Chief Operating Officer, presses the button to cut the first sheet of steel for Queen Mary 2.

March update
73% of steel material ordered.
2 panels (out of 580) completed.
6% of the steel cut.

April update
82% of steel material ordered.
6 panels (out of 580) completed.
11% of the steel cut.

May update
90% of steel material ordered.
7 panels (out of 580) completed.
15% of the steel cut (5,200 tons).

11 June
Cunard announces Maiden Voyage date (12 January 2004) and 2004 schedule for new flagship.

June update
94% of steel material ordered.
62 panels (out of 580) completed.
28% of the steel cut (9,700 tons).

4 July
Keel-laying ceremony takes place.

July Update
98% of steel material ordered.
120 panels (out of 580) completed.
35% of the steel cut (11,800 tons).

8 – 11 August
First block of Queen Mary 2 floats for the first time and moves into the second position of the building dock.

September update
273 panels (out of 580) completed.
70% of the steel cut (23,500 tons).
14 blocks (out of 97) are on board.

October update
430 panels (out of 580) completed.
93% of the steel cut (31,300 tons).
44 blocks (out of 97) are on board.

November update
516 panels (out of 620) completed.
99% of the steel cut (33,400 tons).
49 blocks (out of 98) are on board.

1 December
Queen Mary 2 floats down to the deeper end of the dry dock.

2003

January update
620 panels (out of 620) completed.
100% of the steel cut (33,700 tons).
94 blocks (out of 100) are on board.

5 February
450 crew cabins and 8 balcony cabins have been loaded by this date. About 87% of cabin windows and portholes are installed.

16 March
Mast-stepping ceremony takes place.

21 March
Queen Mary 2 is moved to the fitting out basin.

May update
Approximately 1,000 of the 2,017 passenger and crew cabins have been installed. Installation of funnel and mast completed.

June
The painting of Queen Mary 2's exterior begins.

25 September
Queen Mary 2 takes to the open sea and undergoes her first sea trials.

7 – 11 Nov
Queen Mary 2 undertakes owner's trials.

22 December
Queen Mary 2 is handed over to Cunard.

2004

8 January
Queen Mary 2 is officially named in Southampton.

12 January
Queen Mary 2 departs on her 14-day Maiden Voyage from Southampton to Fort Lauderdale.

Captain Ron Warwick at the Chantiers de l'Atlantique ship yard in Saint-Nazaire, France, as the keel-laying ceremony took place on Queen Mary 2. The ceremony marked the symbolic start of construction of the 1,132ft-long vessel

Queen Mary 2 in numbers...

For the construction of Queen Mary, some thousands of pieces of steel were cut and welded into blocks in specialised workshops.

Her hull is made up of 94 steel blocks (made from 580 panels), some of which weigh more than 600 tons, involving some 1,500 kilometres of welding.

The hull weighs 50,000 tons (more than a school of 330 blue whales) – not to be confused with her gross tonnage, which is 150,000 grt.

At 1,132 feet long, Queen Mary 2 is:

- Five times longer than Cunard's first ship, Britannia (230 ft)
- 113 feet longer than the original Queen Mary (1,019 ft)
- Four football fields in length
- Half as long again as the Canary Wharf Tower is high (800 ft)
- Three times as long as St Paul's Cathedral is high (366 ft)
- Three-and-half times as long as the tower of Big Ben is high (310 ft)
- Longer than 41 London buses (31.5 ft each)
- Twice as long as the Washington Monument is high (555 ft)
- 147 feet longer than the Eiffel Tower is high (984 ft)
- Only 117 feet shorter than the Empire State Building is high
- Over two-and-half times longer than the height of the 'London Eye'
- The length of three blocks on Broadway
- Equal to the height of a 23-storey building (17 decks tower 200 feet above the waterline)

On board there are...

- 1,550 miles (2,500 kilometres) of electric cable
- 310 miles (500 kilometres) of ducts, mains and pipes
- 2,000 bathrooms
- 80,000 lighting points
- 280,000 square yards (250,000 square metres) of fitted carpets
- 144,000 square yards (120,000 square metres) of insulating material
- 3,800 square yards (3,200 square metres) of galleys
- More than 2,500 windows and portholes
- 3,000 telephones
- 8,800 loudspeakers
- 5,000 stairs
- 5,000 fire detectors
- 1,100 fire doors
- 8,350 automatic extinguishers
- 16 polyethylene mooring ropes of 220 metres in length and two 200 metre steel towlines.

And...

- Painters covered an area of 370,000 square yards (550,000 square metres) using 250 tons of paint.
- She measures 237 feet (72 metres) from keel to funnel top.
- With her stern against the Empire State Building, Queen Mary 2 would reach along Fifth Avenue to beyond 38th Street (over four city blocks).
- She covers an area of 3.5 acres
- The total plant is capable of producing nearly 118MW of electricity which is about twice the power of a 100,000-ton conventional cruise ship. This is equal to the power of 1,600 cars.
- Once around Queen Mary 2's 360-degree Promenade Deck is 2034 feet (620 metres) which is well over a third of a mile.
- Her power plant produces sufficient electricity to light a city the size of Southampton (population 200,000).

- Her engines produce 157,000 horsepower – the equivalent of 1,570 family cars (of 100 hp each).
- Her whistle is audible for ten miles.
- With the original Queen Mary, Queen Mary 2 would fill the area of Trafalgar Square.
- Queen Mary 2 can accommodate a fleet of 600 London buses within her 3.5 acre footprint.
- Queen Mary 2's speed of 29.5 knots is double the speed of a Caribbean cruise ship and nearly three times the speed of a blue whale.
- Queen Mary 2 could carry 130 Britannias (Cunard's first ship) within her immense structure.
- The illuminated name positioned where the gas turbines are located is 22 metres long and 2.4 metres high.

QUEEN VICTORIA

The scenes and sounds were reminiscent of a broadcast from an exciting sports event. Clutching his microphone in one white-knuckled hand, and with his other palm firmly on top of his headphones as if a great realisation had dawned, the local radio reporter working in a makeshift media room at the sprawling shipyard near Venice began his piece.

His assignment that cold and damp November day in 2007 was to cover the formal handing over of Cunard's newest ship from her builders at the Marghera shipyard of Italian industrial giant Fincantieri.

"Magnifico! Magnifico! Magnifico!"

He chose his word carefully, and, as it was the only one the arriving British guests heard before being whisked aboard Queen Victoria, those listening felt safe in assuming he had been impressed by what he had seen.

In placing the order for this new Cunarder in December 2004, the Line's parent company Carnival Corporation & plc demonstrated its confidence in both its Cunard brand and the potential to grow its segment of the British market.

Among those inclined to keep a close eye on the timing of such announcements, speculation mounted over the implications for the ageing QE2.

The construction and delivery schedule for Queen Victoria suggested she would enter service as QE2 notched up her 40th anniversary as a Cunarder.

In the event, the sale of QE2 to the Government of Dubai was announced just five months before the new Queen Victoria's maiden voyage, and a mere four months before the announcement of a further new build as the order for Queen Elizabeth was placed with the same Italian contractors.

From their generally chaotic surroundings on the quayside, Cunard's guests slowly made their way up the gangway to judge for themselves just how "magnifico" the new ship was going to be.

Queen Victoria's external lines provided the ship's interior designers with magnificent height and volume to create her public rooms, with grand, elegant yet intimate areas.

The three-storey Grand Lobby sets the tone for the dramatic architecture and design found throughout the ship. The Grand Lobby has become a majestic and powerful focal point, the centre of onboard activity.

It forms the core from which the ship's other public rooms flow, and its architecture is in keeping with the ambiance of Cunard ocean liners of the past while its design also offers the contemporary elegance of a modern-day luxury hotel.

The dramatic triple height ceiling, sweeping staircase and sculpted balconies create an immediate and unmistakable sense of grandeur and arrival. A bronzed-effect sculptural representation of the ship emerging from a sun motif, co-ordinated with a marquetry relief map of the world, graces the staircase landing and is a striking focal point viewable from nearly every part of the Grand Lobby.

1 Connexions™ Conference Centre (Deck 3)	11 Sea View Sauna - Cunard Royal Spa (Deck 9)
2 Cunard Royal Spa & Fitness Centre (Deck 9)	12 Sports Deck (Deck 11)
3 Cunardia Museum (Deck 2)	13 Royal Court Theatre (Decks 1, 2 & 3)
4 Empire Casino (Deck 2)	14 The Grand Lobby
5 Images (Deck 3)	15 The Royal Arcade - Shops (Deck 3)
6 Library (Decks 2 & 3)	16 The Terrace (Deck 11)
7 Hydropool - Cunard Royal Spa (Deck 9)	17 The Zone and Play Zone (Deck 10)
8 Lido Pool - Aft (Deck 9)	18 Whirlpools - Lido Pool - Aft (Deck 9)
9 Pavilion Pool (Deck 9)	19 Whirlpools - Pavilion Pool (Deck 9)
10 Queens Arcade (Deck 2)	20 The Grills Upper Terrace (Deck 12)

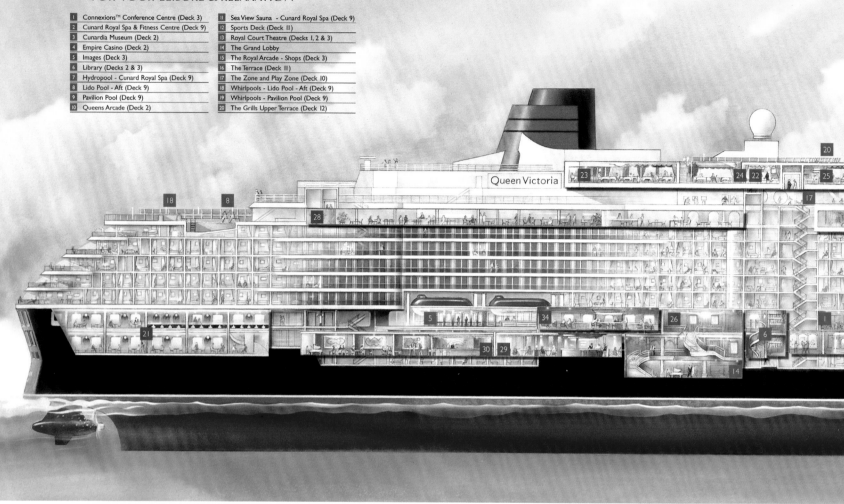

Elsewhere, there is the official maritime portrait of Queen Victoria at sea by Robert Lloyd as well as Victorian and contemporary-sculpted Cunard logos.

An earth tone colour palette of creamy beige, chestnut brown and gold is found throughout, from light mahogany walls and circular hand-woven area rugs to intricately designed marble floors. Here, guests can conduct shipboard business at the Purser's Desk.

Each grade of stateroom or suite is paired with a sea-view restaurant. The restaurants follow a similar pattern to Cunard's other ships, with Grill Rooms for the higher categories and a main restaurant for the deluxe and standard staterooms.

The main Dining Room, the Britannia Restaurant, seats 878 guests, and spans two decks at the stern of the vessel. It evokes memories of classic ocean liner restaurants with sweeping staircases and art deco pillars and arches.

The design of the ship's largest dining room was inspired by the dining car of the Golden Arrow train that linked London to Paris.

The restaurant's Art Deco design is captured in its original artwork, wall features and a combination of authentic finishes including polished wood, bronze, mirror and gold leaf. The room's focal point — an illuminated world globe — at 10 feet tall is a sizable reminder of Cunard's rich history plying the world's oceans. A string quartet or harpist regularly perform at dinner.

The Queens and Princess Grills are in a commanding position at the top of the ship and each features spectacular floor to ceiling panoramic windows.

The forward-facing Grills Lounge is a room ideal for refined afternoon tea, cocktails accompanied by live entertainment. Grill guests have a concierge service based here.

French doors open from each Grill on to The Courtyard

– an exclusive Tuscan-inspired patio area, with a lion-shaped water feature, which accommodates dining al fresco for up to 40 guests, while a wrought iron balustrade stairway leads up to the Upper Grills Terrace – a secluded and exclusive Grills Guests only retreat that's on the ship's uppermost deck.

Queen Victoria offers several alternative dining venues. The 87-seat Verandah Restaurant offers refined elegance. Waterford crystal, Wedgwood china, and Gainsborough silverware add the finishing touches

The 468-seat Lido is a casual, informal dining area that features historic Cunard images that help to create a sophisticated setting for guests to enjoy a wide buffet selection for breakfast, lunch and dinner.

In the evening, the Lido introduces bistro-style dining venues with reserved seating to enjoy menus from around the world.

Café Carinthia is named after a former Cunard ship and offers the style and sophistication of a traditional French patisserie. It is an elegant space highlighted by Art Deco elements in shades of gold, blue and rich bronze.

The café is a favourite haunt of guests from early morning until late evening.

The 59-seat café also has a full bar. Artwork includes maritime painter Stephen Card's commissioned portrait of Carinthia and a series of London maps from a first edition copy of Charles Dickens' London Atlas is also featured.

The Golden Lion pub is the venue for traditional pub food for lunch – from bangers and mash to fish and chips. This is a popular venue, with traditional pub décor – from its beams and traditional pressed metal ceiling tiles, to its antique glass windows and its blackboard menus.

The 830-seat three-deck Royal Court Theatre was designed to capture the grandeur and luxury of the spectacular designs of noted architect Frank Matcham, whose dramatic multi-

tiered theatres made him one of the most prolific theatre designers, with over 80 venues to his name.

Among the Royal Court's most distinguishing features is the collection of 16 West End-style boxes, the first-ever at sea, that frame the stage and afford 32 guests exclusive seating.

The boxes are furnished with graceful armchairs and cocktail tables. A 'Theatre Experience' can be pre-reserved before a show including Veuve Clicquot champagne along with hors d'oeuvres or petit fours served by white-gloved Bell Boys playing their parts as theatre ushers.

The ambience of the Royal Court Theatre is that of a 19th century theatre, with full proscenium arch, rich brocade fabric dressing the walls and a deep red velvet curtain masking the stage.

Queen Victoria's two-deck Queens Room was inspired by Osborne House, Queen Victoria's home on the Isle of Wight, and is redolent of a grand ballroom in a large country house.

This two-deck high room is designed for dancing, cocktail parties and afternoon tea, accompanied by a harpist or string quartet. Crowning the room are two magnificent crystal chandeliers which are reflected in the intricate, backlit, leaded-glass panels which line one wall of this refined, pastel-hued, room.

Murals inspired by the views from Osborne House, cantilevered balconies which overlook the ballroom and are detailed with classically-ornate, curved railings and the popular Victorian practice of 'faux marble' panels complete the décor of this magnificent room. The 1,000 square-foot patterned dance floor is hand-crafted of inlaid wood in light maple.

The 4,000 square foot Royal Arcade was inspired by both the Royal and Burlington Arcades in London and features a grand staircase at the forward end. The light wood panelling contrasts with rich green marbles and gold and white stone textures. The centrepiece of this area is a custom-built, chiming Pillar Clock by the English clockmaker Dent & Co, the clockmaker to HRH Queen Victoria, whose most famous work is Big Ben.

The clock housing is black with gold-leaf lettering and the backlit dial has black Roman numerals.

With its 270-degree views through expansive floor-to-ceiling windows, Hemispheres on Deck 10 is a spectacular nightclub – the most contemporary area on the ship.

The forward facing Commodore Club observation lounge offers sweeping views over the ship's bow. The Commodore Club captures the essence of liner elegance and highlights include 'porthole-style' murals of past Cunard liners and two intricate ship models (QE2 and Cunard Countess) at the entrance.

The traditionally-styled Library offers guests a selection of 6,000 books. This mahogany wood panelled room is one of the most remarkable libraries at sea. Leather sofas and armchairs rest on a carpet embedded with signatures of literary figures, a feature which links in with the Cunard Quote Quest which can be found throughout the ship..

Complementing the Library is a Bookshop offering bestsellers, magazines, postcards and nautically-themed items.

With its retractable glass roof and honeycomb tile-clad walls, The Winter Garden is Queen Victoria's indoor/outdoor relaxation area. With colonial style ceiling fans, rattan furniture and an appropriate scattering of greenery, this is a popular place to enjoy afternoon tea, juices from the Juice Bar, or strawberries and cream.

Queen Victoria offers a range of 13 bars and clubs including:

A nautical atmosphere in the 77-seat Chart Room featuring sand-blasted maps with sea views, glass cases displaying ship models and maritime artefacts, Cunard items on display include shipbuilding receipts, a 1930s Cunard sailor cap, and two sailor-made models of Queen Mary and Caronia. Balustrade railings in this room are modelled on those in the First-Class Dining Room on the original Queen Mary.

The Midships Lounge boasts four 1929 Art Deco prints by Beresford Egan as well as two contemporary bronze sculptures by Erte.

ConneXions Conference Centre and Internet Centre includes an education centre featuring a flexible classroom venue for programmes including Computer Training, Navigation and Art and Wine Tasting.

Child facilities on board include The Play Zone and The Zone. These spaces feature the very latest equipment for children of all ages, a permanent staff with trained nannies and nursery nurses and there's an indoors and outdoors playing area.

The Cunard Royal Spa and Fitness Centre features the latest spa and beauty treatments for both men and women, as well as a hydro-pool and thermal suite. Forward of the Spa is an expansive gymnasium and aerobics area with state-of-the-art cardiovascular fitness equipment including inclining treadmills and bikes complete with their own personal LCD television screens.

In addition to the large hydro-pool in the Spa, there are two outdoor swimming pools and four whirlpools for guests to enjoy on the open decks.

QUEEN ELIZABETH

Alighting from the splendidly rickety Pier Train to board the Hythe Ferry late on a Sunday afternoon in the early autumn of 2010, passengers cupped their hands around their ears to catch the strains of music reaching them across Southampton Water.

Like contestants in the music round of a television quiz show, heads lowered and brows furrowed as they tried to identify what they could hear.

The impromptu 'name that tune' started with Zadok the Priest, moved to the opening bars of the National Anthem and carried on with Jerusalem (specially arranged by Cunard's musical director in residence Anthony Inglis) before the Bournemouth Symphony Orchestra, led by Gonzalo Acosta, put in a rousing Pomp and Circumstance.

There is no mistaking the Cunard playlist. Forming the backdrop for this stop/start open air performance was the impressive form of the gleaming new, 91,000-ton Queen Elizabeth, ropes fast alongside Southampton's Ocean Terminal.

A little less than 24 hours after the musicians went through their paces at rehearsal in a specially-built quayside theatre and auditorium, Her Majesty the Queen would be invited to smash a jeroboam of Cunard Graves, Baron Philippe de Rothschild, 2009, against the bow of the ship bearing her name.

It was to be the start of another new chapter in Cunard Line history, notable for the fact that Her Majesty was returning to Southampton to name a new Cunarder just six years after she had named Queen Mary 2 in one of the most spectacular ceremonies of its kind ever staged.

As a 12-year-old Princess Elizabeth, she was present when her mother named the Queen Elizabeth in 1938. Since then she has launched Caronia (1947), Queen Elizabeth 2 (1967) and Queen Mary 2 (2004)

Each of these events, together with countless others involving other members of the Royal Family down the decades, represent a unique aspect of Cunard heritage.

Her Majesty enjoying a tour of Queen Elizabeth with Captain Chris Wells on her return to Southampton in October 2010

Opposite, clockwise from top left: Queen Elizabeth, in 1938, launches the giant Cunard liner bearing her name at Clydebank; the then Princess Elizabeth with Lieutenant Philip Mountbatten, saluting beside her, watches Caronia slide down into the water during her launching at John Brown's shipyard in 1947; Her Majesty is greeted by Commodore Ron Warwick on the bridge of the Queen Mary 2 liner in Southampton before naming the £550 million vessel in front of more than 2,000 guests in 2004. It was the first time the Queen had named a Cunard ship since the launch in 1967 of the QE2, an event also pictured

Under clear blue skies and in dazzling autumn sunshine on the afternoon of Monday, 11 October, 2010, there was no mistaking Her Majesty's delight in performing this latest duty.

During a tour of the new vessel with the Master, Captain Chris Wells, Her Majesty was invited to sound the whistle from the bridge, jumping slightly as the booming sound reverberated across Southampton, and smiling broadly when the audience in the quayside grandstand below cheered loudly. After the Pomp and Ceremony, the ship hosted a Gala Dinner before final preparations for her Maiden Voyage to Iberia and the Canaries.

Sister ships Queen Victoria and Queen Elizabeth share the same hull design. Many of the public rooms are also common to both, although Queen Elizabeth does not have a Chart Room, its space taken by an additional restaurant for Britannia Club guests.

Additional outdoor sports facilities including croquet lawns also feature on Queen Elizabeth. Extra suites (some named after Knighted Cunard Line Commodores) have been added to the accommodation layout used on the newer of the two sisters.

Her Majesty Queen Elizabeth names the ship and, right, she is pictured alongside Captain Chris Wells in the Grand Lobby

ART OF THE SEA

Stunning paintings from internationally-acclaimed marine artist Robert Lloyd, featuring scenes on the Mersey, have charted much of Cunard's history

One of Robert Lloyd's masterpieces, featuring the paddle steamer Britannia alongside the 150,000-ton flagship Queen Mary 2 at Liverpool, became the focal point of a special event to launch plans for Cunard's 175th anniversary celebrations.

The painting was unveiled at a ceremony in the Cunard Building in April 2014 by Mayor of Liverpool Joe Anderson, assisted by Cunard Marketing Director Angus Struthers and the artist.

Robert Lloyd's interest in the sea started during his childhood in Wirral, the peninsular formed by the Mersey on one side and the River Dee on the other.

"During school summer holidays I used to go with my mother to New Brighton promenade to watch the ships going in and out of Liverpool. This was in the late 1970s and early 80s and there really wasn't much to see apart from the occasional coaster or Isle of Man Steam Packet ferry. If I was lucky, I would see an ACL container ship coming in or leaving," he recalls.

Artist Robert Lloyd next to his painting which was commissioned to mark the 175th anniversary celebrations and (below) the QE2 leaving Liverpool

Opposite: The Lusitania (top) and Sylvania and Britannic at Liverpool

"I was fascinated even at that age, I had been on a trip up the Manchester Ship Canal on one of the Mersey Ferries, and had taken some photos at the oil terminal at Eastham of a tanker.

"Then my art teacher set a project to do a painting for a competition at school so I decided to paint that tanker. It won the competition, £10 I think I won, and it was exhibited at a local library."

Growing up on a peninsular influenced the young artist.

"Being surrounded by sea on three sides on Wirral obviously had a major influence on my interest in shipping and the sea. From my bedroom window I could see the Bar Light ship which I suppose was about 15 miles away. I could see the ships passing and anchored and those same thoughts used to come to mind. I could also see Hilbre Island and the Dee Estuary and would often see small coasters and occasionally a Trinity House Tender negotiating the twisting channels out of the Estuary.

The Mersey Ferries also proved a popular draw for the youngster.

"I would often sail back and forth on the Mersey Ferries; windy rough days were the best, rolling all over the place. I always enjoyed rough weather, and still do. I recall a particularly rough crossing to the Isle of Man on a family holiday. It was on one of the old steamers. It was probably only a force six or seven but the ferry was rolling and pitching all over the place.

"Most of the passengers seemed to have disappeared, there was hardly anyone on deck. I loved it. The wind was moaning in the rigging and the spray was coming right across the decks. It was for me a wonderful experience although it did teach me to carefully observe the other passengers; I was careful to always stay well up wind of anyone who looked even slightly green!"

As the time to leave school approached Robert was considering a career at sea.

"I had decided to pursue a career at sea. However, my careers teacher suggested that perhaps I would have a better future if I pursued a career in art and went to Art College instead. So that is what I ended up doing. I was studying graphics and illustration and then went on to study industrial and three dimensional design at a college outside London. At this point all thoughts of the sea had pretty much disappeared and after leaving college I joined an advertising agency working for the likes of Virgin, Proctor & Gamble, Phillip Morris and Chrysalis producing brochures, record covers and so on."

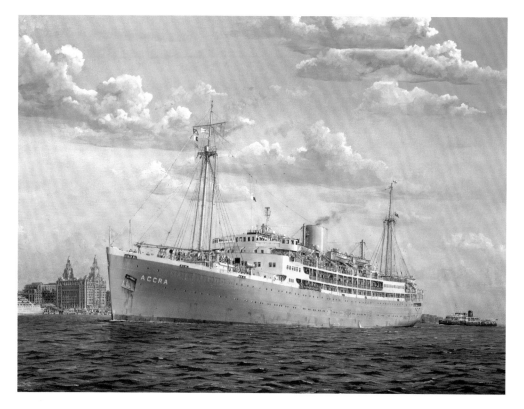

Among the clients of the advertising agency was P&O Ferries.

"Knowing my interest in fine art painting, they asked me to produce a painting of one of their new ferries, the Pride of Portsmouth. Then they commissioned two more and made a number of introductions to other shipping companies who all seemed interested in having me produce paintings for them. I eventually gave up working in advertising and started to paint full time."

Over the years he has painted a wide range of shipping subjects for companies, museums and individuals all over the world. The subjects have ranged from oil tankers to oil rigs, cruise ships and liners to ferries and container ships.

"Probably my most challenging commission to date has been a series of paintings rather than one individual painting," he reveals.

"For more than two years I was working on a series of 40 paintings for a company called Qatargas. They had under construction what was the largest ever peacetime order for ships. To give a comparison, Cunard's Queen Victoria weighs 90,000 tons, not small by any measure, but these gas carriers weigh in at 220,000 tons and are over 300 meters in length.

"They are Liquid Natural Gas carriers and although each had some technical differences, they were essentially very similar in appearance. The challenge was not only the number of paintings to complete but to ensure that each painting showed a different view and background. That's easy enough for five paintings but a great deal of thought and research has to be put in for 40!"

The relative scale of Britannia and Queen Mary 2 presented a particular challenge for Robert.

"It is very difficult to find any images of Britannia, if not impossible, but dimensioned general arrangement drawings are freely available so one can gather the relative difference in size between the two vessels," he explains.

"As we wanted to make Queen Mary 2 look as impressive as possible whilst still showing the iconic Liverpool waterfront clearly, she would have to be pictured quite 'head on' as opposed to a broadside.

"If the Britannia was shown broadside, too much of the Queen Mary 2 would be lost behind, so I decided to complete her almost head on as well. This then makes a very dynamic view and gives a good sense of the sheer scale of Cunard's flagship.

"It is also well-known that the Britannia would herself fit within the Britannia Restaurant on the Queen Mary 2."

Attention to detail and accuracy is a hallmark of Robert's work. His depictions of Liverpool waterfront and shipping on the River Mersey is not limited to Cunarders.

"I have completed a large number of paintings both historical and modern which feature the River Mersey and the Pier Head in particular. These have ranged from Taiwanese bulk carriers, old cargo passenger ships and of course many of the old Alfred Holt Blue Funnel Line ships."

When a particular work has been commissioned, Robert follows a carefully refined process to create the finished painting.

"I start with a general thumbnail sketch to get the basic positions of the key elements then gradually work it up to a more finished sketch. When the proportions look visually accurate, I then get the calculator out and start working out exact scales and dimensions so it not only looks right but is also mathematically correct. Sometimes you have to make adjustments by eye to ensure it 'looks right'.

"This first stage, the pencil layout sketch, is important not only to ensure the technical accuracy and general appearance of the painting, but also to allow the customer to see exactly what the finished painting will look like. Also, for me, it helps to see what will work and what won't.

"Sometimes I will be three-quarters of the way through a sketch and it becomes apparent that as a full size painting it just won't look right. Many artists often skip this stage entirely but end up having to review later and move elements on the actual painting but to my mind, this would look scrappy. Often you can see on a finished painting where this has been done. Initial sketches also avoid the possibility of the customer asking for major changes to the finished painting."

Despite his widespread travels across the oceans and to the world's ports, Liverpool, and its historic waterfront, always remain in Robert's mind.

"Having spent so much of my childhood on the banks of the Mersey it has of course always been very much in my mind. Some of the first paintings I completed were of vessels on the Mersey and it taught me the value of depicting water, particularly its colours, accurately. With the strong tidal flows at the mouth of the Mersey there is obviously a lot of sediment churned up, especially when the tide is going out. It makes the water appear quite brown. One of the first paintings I did

was of the North West Water vessel Gilbert J. Fowler. Not really knowing better, I painted the water a greenish blue. The customer then asked me if I had ever seen the river that colour. The answer of course was no! An important lesson. This has always stayed in my mind, and now many people say my seas are noticeable for their accuracy. In many ways, I think this is due to that one experience."

Many customers and collectors describe his work as "photographic" in its detail.

"If this reputation stays with me I would hope that in years to come people could use my work for reference safe in the knowledge that what I show is indeed an accurate depiction," he says.

Robert occasionally travels as Cunard's "artist in residence" working on board the Three Queens to complete unique records of chosen voyages.

"I very much enjoy working on the Cunard ships. It is always entertaining, sometimes tiring but never boring. Working on a ship of course is far from ideal from an artist's point of view. On a recent trip across the Atlantic I had to complete a painting in six days and five of those days were stormy to say the least. When the ship pitched into a wave you braced yourself, but as long as the movement of the vessel doesn't involve shuddering or sudden slamming, then you get used to it. The same cannot be said for the passengers who stumble in to you or the painting. That is a constant worry."

From his collection of works featuring Cunard ships, Robert has two favourites.

"One has to be 'Coming Home' depicting the Queen Elizabeth 2 arriving at Southampton for the last time. It was a large painting but was unveiled by the Queen who subsequently asked for it to be made into a jigsaw puzzle of about 2,500 pieces. I sometimes wonder if she ever completed it. The painting was then presented to the City of Southampton by the Duke of Edinburgh a few months later. My other favourite painting was quite a bit larger and features the Queen Mary 2, Queen Victoria and QE2 at Southampton. It was quite a technical challenge having three ships together in one painting but worked very well. It now hangs in the Commodore Club on board the Queen Elizabeth."

HRH the Duke of Edinburgh unveiled another of Robert's paintings on board Queen Mary 2 during a visit to mark the ship's first decade in service in May 2014. "He was interested in the work and the detail of the ship," says Robert.

His association with Cunard started after a meeting with retired Commodore Ron Warwick. "I was first introduced to

Robert Lloyd shows Her Majesty his portrait of Queen Elizabeth 2 and, opposite, the Duke of Edinburgh unveiling a 10th anniversary commission showing Queen Mary 2 at night

Cunard by Commodore Ron Warwick. I had just completed a painting for him of the QE2. He was master at the time and he invited me on board whilst the ship was in Southampton."

"My first commission directly from Cunard was presented to Margaret Thatcher to commemorate QE2's part in the Falkland War. I believe she had this painting hung in her drawing room at home."

The artist believes the history and heritage of Cunard Line is unique – and feels honoured to be making his own special contribution.

"Over the years I have met a great many people not only who work for Cunard but also have an interest and indeed a passion for the history and heritage of Cunard which cannot help but rub off on you.

"Mention most shipping company names and you are greeted by a blank look. Mention Cunard and everyone knows what you are talking about. I always feel deeply honoured to be able to contribute to the company's long and rich heritage with the paintings and it is of course wonderful to be asked to do so as part of the 175th anniversary."

Some of the men and women of the Mersey (left to right): River Pilots James Smart and Chris Booker; Cruise Liverpool's Cruise and Operations Manager Angie Redhead and Marine Operations Manager Bob Swift; Ship's Agent Katy Lawler of Denholm Wilhelmsen

MAKING MARITIME & HISTORY

When Queen Elizabeth 2 arrived at the Liverpool Cruise Terminal on a wet and windy morning in September 2007, the final piece of a complex jigsaw dropped into place.

The arrival and safe handling of the most famous ship in the world alongside at Liverpool declared the city's new cruise facility open for business.

Since that auspicious start, the Cruise Liverpool team, led by Cruise and Operations Manager Angie Redhead, has handled more than 175 cruise vessel calls at the berth.

Preparing for the QE2's arrival that day brought numerous challenges as construction of the berth had itself been an ambitious project.

A measure of how close the calls to be ready by 21 September were was evident a few days after QE2 left the berth and sailed for her homeport of Southampton.

The pomp and ceremony of the Royal Opening seemed a distant memory as construction workers, cranes and tugs returned to the berth to remove a large section and return it to dry dock for further work.

The removal process was reversed when work on the concrete section was completed at Cammell Laird's Birkenhead shipyard and it was towed safely back across the river to be reinstalled.

Once it was back in place, engineers oversaw the re-fitting of the foot bridge linking that end of the berth to the river wall at Princes Parade. The bridge had stood forlornly on nearby wasteland after it was detached and hoisted away to allow the removal of the pontoon.

"My recollection of planning for QE2's first call in 2007 is the pressure of completing the construction of the new terminal in time," says Angie Redhead. "Like any major project, there were challenges. Horrendous weather and challenging tidal conditions had set the project back somewhat and we were desperately trying to gain ground."

In the intervening eight years Liverpool's cruise operation has grown from strength to strength, landing coveted national awards for the city as a destination and international recognition for the Cruise and Operations Manager.

The influential Cruise Critic UK online forum declared Liverpool Best UK Port of Call in 2013 and 2014, and, in the same year, the Women's International Shipping and Trade Association made Angie Redhead its Personality of the Year.

"I was extremely honoured, humbled and flattered to be named winner," she says. "It means a huge amount to me. I was delighted to bring the Award home to Liverpool."

Her success marked the first time in 14 years that the International Award had been secured for the UK.

Seeking to shun the spotlight, the Cruise and Operations Manager is keen to underline the part played by others in the successful development of Liverpool's cruise offer.

"Through huge public support and partnership working within our maritime 'village' we have collectively made Liverpool Cruise Terminal the huge success it is today," she says.

Each of the 175 calls that have been handled since 2007 has required dedication and commitment from a wide and diverse range of individuals working on the Mersey and in the port. Liverpool Cruise Terminal Marine Operations Manager Bob Swift has worked on the Mersey for 47 years – 41 one of them as a Pilot making him the longest serving there has been on the Mersey.

He joined the Cruise Terminal team in 2008 and provides a critical, expert link between the operations teams at the world's cruise lines, the river Pilots and the Captains, officers and crews of visiting ships. For every cruise ship arrival and departure he helps plan and deliver, he brings with him experience of handling more than 6,000 vessels in the Mersey, including large oil tankers and bulk carriers.

He cites the first arrival of Queen Mary 2 alongside at Liverpool as one of his most memorable events since becoming Marine Operations Manager.

"The ship arrived on a strong flood tide and had to turn through 180 degrees before dropping in towards the Cruise Liner Terminal. The turn was executed far more quickly than I could have imagined and was a magnificent sight. She berthed alongside the Terminal perfectly. Parallel, flat and with almost no weight."

The Pilot assigned to QM2 that day was Captain Chris Booker, the senior Event Pilot for the Three Queens salute to Liverpool. He has been involved in the detailed planning for the 175th Anniversary events on the Mersey for almost 18 months.

"Meticulous planning by the Liverpool Pilots, involving input from all parties, is crucial to a smooth but exciting performance on the day. It promises to be a once in a lifetime experience for everyone involved," he says.

Fellow Liverpool Pilot James Smart says he feels privileged to work on the river. "I had a fantastic career with P&O Princess, but the opportunity to join Liverpool Pilots came about and I feel very lucky to be in this job," he says. "I really enjoy the satisfaction of sailing a large ship in and out of Liverpool."

The main challenge facing Liverpool Pilots is the size of the tidal range – and weather conditions so close to the Irish Sea. There are around 9,000 acts of pilotage in Liverpool each year and, on average each Pilot is responsible for around 185 ship movements annually.

Much of Liverpool's success in attracting and developing its cruise business also involves numerous other port-based companies and suppliers working together to meet the needs of the cruise lines and their visiting ships.

Katy Lawler is a ship's agent with one of the biggest operations of its kind in the UK – Denholm Wilhelmsen.

Her duties can take her to the Cruise Terminal at any hour of the day or night depending on the schedules and requirements of her company's clients. As well as playing a pivotal role in the logistics of servicing and supplying visiting vessels, her work often involves sharing the experiences enjoyed ashore by visiting guests.

"I think the passengers are just so charmed with the city. Every time that they come in, there is just so much to see and do and they are so surprised at how beautiful the city is and how much it has changed, and for the better as well," she says.

QE2's historic arrival in September 2007 marked the start of an astonishing chapter in the city's maritime history and in 2015 her sisters Queen Mary 2, Queen Victoria and Queen Elizabeth write their own – together with the men and women of the Mersey.

NEW LEASE OF LIFE FOR CUNARD BUILDING

Cunard built its foundations in Liverpool and on the River Mersey in the 19th century, and the relationship still continues with new vigour

The beginning of another chapter in the 175-year association between Cunard and Liverpool started on the 16 April, 2014, on the steps of the famous Pier Head building bearing the founder's name.

It was here, 47 years after Cunard moved its operations from Liverpool to the United States and Southampton, that first details of how the entire fleet would return to its spiritual home were announced.

The grand, ground floor former Booking Hall at the Cunard Building was the venue for a special presentation setting out the plans for the spectacular One Magnificent City salute to Liverpool.

Mayor Joe Anderson welcomed Cunard Marketing Director Angus Struthers to the former headquarters of the most famous shipping line in the world – with a resplendent Cunard Bell Boy in attendance.

The event also marked the unveiling of a specially commissioned painting depicting the paddle steamer Britannia, which first sailed from Liverpool to North America in 1840, and the current Cunard flagship Queen Mary 2, together on the River Mersey in front of the Cunard Building.

From the very beginning, the British and North American Royal Mail Steam Packet Company – thankfully abbreviated to become universally known as Cunard Line – had its headquarters in Liverpool.

Although Samuel Cunard himself was based in Halifax, Nova Scotia, one of his two partners was already established as a ship manager in Liverpool.

A pivotal point in Cunard's history was the mass emigration from Europe to the United States, and travel arrangements were prepared and managed from the Liverpool offices. The scale of Cunard's Liverpool-based operations were such that emigrants from central Europe could book their complete train and ferry requirements to get them to the banks of the Mersey to board their ship for the New World.

And by this time, some Americans had availed themselves of the opportunity to cross the Atlantic to Liverpool with Cunard, board another of the Line's ships on the Mersey and sail off to the Mediterranean to take the Grand Tour.

After another 50 years or so of expansion and solid growth, Cunard was ready to commission its own landmark headquarters building.

The Cunard Building was built on the site of George's Dock. Work on this port facility had started in 1767 and by 1900 it was too small for the generation of steamships operating to and from Liverpool and was closed.

Liverpool's renowned Three Graces now occupy the site of the former dock and were themselves the foundation of the City's successful bid for UNESCO World Heritage Site status, inscribed in July 2004.

The Cunard Building was the last of the three to be built – the Port of Liverpool being first, followed by the Liver.

Designed to reflect the strength and style of the floating palaces at sea, the building required a construction project on a massive scale. The building is based on the form of a Papal Palace in Rome and used 180,000 cubic feet of Portland Stone and 50,000 cubic feet of Italian marble inside.

The old dock walls – still visible in a section of the basement – were reinforced with 700,000 cubic feet of concrete to keep the Mersey at bay.

The huge building's floor space could accommodate 250,000 people standing shoulder to shoulder and the corridors, stairways and public rooms were lavishly decorated.

More than 1,000 Cunard staff worked in the building, from hydrographers mapping the world's tides to the experimental chef who tried out new recipes on employees before they were unleashed on the passengers.

On the ground floor was the enormous and magnificent pillared ticket hall and lounge for First Class passengers. Second and third-class passengers were dealt with in the first basement – including, for emigrants, compulsory medical examinations.

Shields on the riverside elevation acknowledge the period when the building was constructed, being the arms of countries allied in the Great War – Britain, France, Russia, Italy, Japan, Belgium, Serbia and Montenegro. At each corner is the shield of the Cunard company, supported by an eagle – each weighing 43 tons. And above each third floor window are the arms of the principal passenger ports in the United Kingdom – Liverpool, Bristol, Southampton, Plymouth, Falmouth, Hull, Portsmouth, Newcastle, Glasgow, Leith, Aberdeen, Dundee and Queenstown.

Below, Mayor of Liverpool Joe Anderson, left, together with Cunard director Angus Struthers, inside the Cunard Building

Historic decisions having a bearing on the company's future were taken on the fifth floor – many being ratified in the splendid Boardroom which remains today. This floor was also home to the naval architects' department, and it was here that designs and drawings for many of the most famous Cunarders ever built – including the record-breaking Queen Elizabeth 2 – were conceived and laid out.

Cunard moved into its prestigious new headquarters, its third and last in Liverpool, in June 1916, and remained there for more than 50 years. The prime waterfront location allowed the company's directors to observe the comings

goings of their prized assets – the ships – from their own Boardroom. But in 1936 a shift started which was to see the firm's allegiance switch away from Liverpool.

In that year Queen Mary entered service and despite having Liverpool cast on her stern as her port of registry, she was too big to enter the Mersey and never even visited. Her maiden voyage started on 27 May, 1936, from Southampton. Change was upon Cunard and Liverpool.

The ship was based in the south coast port, where other Cunard operations had already been moved, and from where her sister Queen Elizabeth later started services. Cunard Directors in Liverpool could no longer gaze upon the flags of their fleet from their Boardroom.

Despite the shift south, Cunard Building was the focal point for the creation and launch into service of the most famous and successful liner in the company's history Queen Elizabeth 2. Though the ship came to life on the banks of the Clyde at Glasgow, hers was a gestation nurtured in Liverpool.

By 1967, with the new ship launched, the focus of Cunard activity had well and truly shifted away from Liverpool to

Southampton and, after 128 years on the banks of the Mersey, Cunard's head office moved to New York and its operational base to Southampton.

Liverpool, though, remains the spiritual home of the most famous passenger shipping line ever launched.

No other city in the world will ever share such a prominent place in the firm's history.

The Rector of Liverpool, the Reverend Dr Crispin Pailing, left, and The Reverend David Baverstock are pictured in front of the memorial panels at Liverpool Parish Church honouring the lives of Cunard employees who fell during two world wars

AT SEA IN PEACE AND IN WAR

Cunard workers were among those who fell when the country went to war but a memorial ensures they will never be forgotten

Memorial stones honouring the sacrifice made in the two world wars by Cunard personnel were once a prominent feature of the public spaces at the company's former headquarters in Cunard Building.

These were transferred and later re-dedicated at Liverpool Parish Church, Our Lady and Saint Nicholas, in July 1990. A large and striking memorial remains outside the building facing the River Mersey.

It was seven years after the end of hostilities in the Second World War, on Wednesday, 17 September, 1952, that memorial panels recording the names and service details of sea going officers and shore staff lost in the conflict were unveiled. The ceremony was performed by the Company Chairman, Mr Frederic Alan Bates.

1939 1945

UNVEILING
OF
MEMORIAL PANELS

BY THE CHAIRMAN, MR. F. A. BATES, M.C., A.F.C., D.L.

WEDNESDAY 17th SEPTEMBER 1952.

CUNARD BUILDING, LIVERPOOL

More than 1,000 people were killed when the Cunard liner Lusitania, top, was torpedoed by Germans on 7 May, 1915, off the Irish coast. Left, some of the vessel's lifeboats

1939　1945

IN MEMORY OF THE SEAGOING OFFICERS
AND SHORE STAFF WHO LOST THEIR LIVES
IN THE SECOND WORLD WAR

PAVEY, D. L.		SHARP, R. R.D.	
FLYING OFFICER	R.A.F.	COMMANDER	R.N.R. (RETD.)
		CAPTAIN	S.S. LACONIA
PEARCE, J. H.			
CHEF	S.S. LACONIA	SMITH, S. J.	
		LIEUTENANT (E) R.N.R.	H.M.S. TYNWALD
PEARSE, J.			
CHEF	S.S. LANCASTRIA	SOLLAS, A. E.	
		2ND ASSISTANT PURSER	S.S. LACONIA
PHIPPS, S. H.			
JUNIOR 2ND ENGINEER	S.S. LACONIA	STEELE, G. R.D.	
		LIEUT-COMMANDER	R.N.R. (RETD.)
PICKERSGILL, R. W.		CHIEF OFFICER	S.S. LACONIA
LIEUTENANT R.N.R.	H.M.S. ALCANTARA		
		STOKES, C. H.	
PORTER, C. E.		JUNIOR 2ND OFFICER	S.S. LACONIA
JUNIOR ASSISTANT PURSER	S.S. LANCASTRIA		
		TAGGART, H. W.	
PURSLOW, G. C.		LIEUT-COMMANDER R.N.R.	H.M.S. VOLTAIRE
M.B., Ch.B., M.R.C.S., L.R.C.P.			
SURGEON	S.S. LACONIA	TIDMAN, B. A.	
		SERGEANT PILOT	R.A.F.
REES, E. D.S.C. R.D.			
COMMODORE 2ND CLASS R.N.R.	H.M.S. EAGLET	THOMPSON, M. P.	
		LIEUTENANT R.N.R.	H.M.S. CURACOA
RELPH, E. W.			
LIEUT-COMMANDER (E) R.N.R.	H.M.S. ESK	TONE, J. W.	
		LIEUT-COMMANDER R.N.R.	H.M.S. REGISTAN
RICHARDSON, F.			
PAYMASTER SUB-LIEUTENANT	R.N.R.	WEST, P.	

Just some of the names which feature on the memorial panels, which were transferred from the Cunard Building to Liverpool Parish Church, pictured top left, after the shipping company left the city in 1967

A communication to staff, including those at sea, issued later recorded the following: "At the Head Office of the Company, Cunard Building, Liverpool, in the presence of relatives, Directors of the Company, and members of the sea-going and shore staffs, Mr. F. A. Bates, M.C., A.F.C., D.L., Chairman of the Cunard Steam-Ship Company Limited, unveiled two panels in memory of the sea-going officers and permanent shore staff of the Company who lost their lives through enemy action in the second world war.

"The ceremony was opened by a senior apprentice of the Company, Cadet T. J. S. Whitehead, asking permission of the Chairman to lower to half-mast the ensign flown by the 'AQUITANIA' on her last voyage, which now adjoins the Memorial Panels near the western entrance to the Company's General Office on the ground floor of Cunard Building. The assembly stood while the flag was lowered, and the General Manager of the Company, Mr. F. H.

Clockwise from top left: The Atlantic Conveyor leaving the River Mersey; the ship just before she joined the task force in the South Atlantic; the Lancastria pictured before and after she was sunk in 1940, sending at least 4,000 people to their deaths, and the Aquitania in 'dazzle ship' livery

Aquitania in the Straits of Gibraltar after bringing sailors to reinforce the Royal Navy's Mediterranean fleet there in 1940

Dawson, C.B.E., M.C., after explaining the purpose of the gathering, asked the Chairman to unveil the panels, which the Chairman did after paying tribute in appropriate and moving words to those whose names are inscribed on them.

"A short silence was then observed, after which the Chairman and the General Manager laid wreaths at the foot of the panels, and the ceremony closed with the raising to mast-head of the 'AQUITANIA'S' ensign.

"The Memorial panels are of green Italian marble from Aosta, and their white surrounds are of Italian Statuary Vein marble from Carrara.

"The architects were Messrs. Willink and Dod, FF.R.I.B.A., and the panels were supplied and inscribed by Messrs John Stubbs (Marble and Quartzite) Ltd., and erected by Messrs. W. Whitby & Sons.

"Thirty-one names are inscribed on the panel on the southern side of the General Office, and thirty on the panel on the northern side."

The panels were rededicated at the Parish Church in 1990.

As well as marking the 175th anniversary of the departure of Britannia from Liverpool bound for North America, 2015 also marks the 33rd anniversary of the loss of Cunard Line's Liverpool-registered container ship Atlantic Conveyor during the 1982 Falklands War.

Twelve lives, including that of the ship's Master Captain Ian North, were lost in the aftermath of an Exocet missile attack that struck at 3.41pm on the afternoon of 25 May 1982.

The vessel, requisitioned, or Ship Taken Up From Trade, by the Ministry of Defence, had joined the South Atlantic Task Force after sailing from the Royal Seaforth Container Terminal at Liverpool.

The anniversary of the loss falls on the same day as the current Cunard fleet will salute Liverpool in May 2015.

A special service to mark both the sinking of the Atlantic Conveyor and the sacrifice of other Cunard sea-going and shore staff in the two world wars, is being planned at Liverpool Parish Church.

The former Cunard flagship Queen Elizabeth 2, left, with Queen Mary 2 and Queen Victoria in Southampton. The current fleet meets in Liverpool, above, in 2015

TIME TO
& CELEBRATE

As befits the spiritual home, Liverpool takes centre stage for
celebrations to mark Cunard's 175th anniversary of its first ship,
Britannia, setting sail from the River Mersey in July 1840

Britannia inaugurated the first-ever regularly-scheduled service across the Atlantic and every year without fail since then, in peace and war, Cunard ships have crossed and re-crossed the Atlantic.

Cunard's flagship Queen Mary 2 will recreate history when she sails from Liverpool on 4 July, 2015, following in the wake of Britannia which left the city 175 years earlier to the day. This will also be the first time since January 1968 that passengers have boarded a Cunard ship at Liverpool to sail to America.

The 10-night crossing from Liverpool will call at Halifax and Boston just like Britannia, and will conclude in New York on 14 July, 2015.

Some 175 years after the inauguration of Cunard's transatlantic service from Liverpool, the current fleet will salute the company's spiritual home.

From 24 to 26 May, 2015, Liverpool will play host to the three largest Cunard ships ever built in an historic, three-day event.

Queen Mary 2 will arrive in Liverpool on Sunday, 24 May, and make her first ever overnight stay in the city, berthed in sight of the Cunard Building.

The following morning, on Monday, 25 May, Queen Elizabeth and Queen Victoria will sail into the city and for a time all three ships of the Cunard fleet will line up on the Mersey in a spectacle that is expected to draw huge crowds. Over a million people saw Queen Elizabeth 2 sail into Liverpool for the first time in July 1990.

Queen Mary 2 will then take her leave and sail out of Liverpool as Queen Elizabeth berths at the City of Liverpool Cruise Terminal, where she will remain until late that night. Queen Victoria, meanwhile, will anchor in the Mersey.

Late in the evening of Monday, 25 May, Queen Elizabeth will set sail and Queen Victoria will then take the berth and remain there overnight and for the following day, Tuesday, 26 May.

Accommodating the three largest vessels ever to make up the Cunard fleet simultaneously in the Mersey has required meticulous and detailed planning.

A series of carefully choreographed ship movements will take place in various parts of the Mersey.

The complex marine operations plan was prepared by a team including the Commodore of the Cunard Fleet Captain Christopher Rynd, Captain Steve Gallimore, the Port of Liverpool Harbour Master and Captain Chris

Celebratory fireworks are set off in honour of Queen Mary 2. Right, Commodore Christopher Rynd and, opposite, another view of the former fleet in Southampton in 2014

Booker, Chairman of Liverpool Pilotage Association and Senior River Pilot for the event. Specially-created computer programmes for the local Pilots' sophisticated simulator were used to plot the precise positions of the three ships and each of their manoeuvres during the event.

Commodore Rynd said: "With the unique backdrop of Liverpool's world-famous waterfront, and the capacity on both sides of the Mersey to accommodate tens of thousands of spectators, I believe this will be a most spectacular gathering of the Three Queens.

"I am excited by the prospect of bringing the Fleet to its spiritual home and I am impressed by the level of engagement and collaboration between the partners involved and required to make it all possible."

Captain Steve Gallimore said: "The sight of the Cunard Queens together in relatively close proximity off Pier Head and elsewhere in the river will create a striking and lasting impression for spectators and those seeing TV coverage all over the world. The Mersey is a challenging environment in

which to move ships the size of the Cunard Queens. This makes the detailed planning and co-ordination involving the Commodore so critical."

Captain Chris Booker said: "Our river simulator, and the input we are receiving from the Cunard Captains, is invaluable in helping us plan and prepare for this event. It promises to be a once in a lifetime experience for everyone involved and spectating on 25 May, 2015."

The 25 May three-ship event features as a highlight of three very different cruise itineraries.

Queen Mary 2 is on 10-night 'British Isles – Liverpool Salute' voyage from Southampton and taking in Cobh, Dublin, Glasgow, Oban and Guernsey.

Queen Elizabeth completes a 16-night 'Baltic – Liverpool Salute' cruise departing Southampton and calling at Oslo, Copenhagen, Stockholm, Tallinn, St Petersburg, Warnemunde and Kirkwall.

Queen Victoria offers a six-night 'Liverpool Salute' voyage from Southampton calling at St Peter Port with an overnight stop at Liverpool before returning to Southampton

A little more than two weeks before the spectacular salute to Liverpool, the world will remember the 100th anniversary of the sinking of the former Cunard flagship Lusitania – torpedoed on 7 May, 1915, while en-route from New York to Liverpool.

The ship sank approximately 14 miles off the Old Head of Kinsale in Ireland. In all, Cunard lost 22 ships during the First World War, including Carpathia which had rescued all of the survivors of the Titanic.

This special seven-night cruise by Queen Victoria will commemorate the loss of Lusitania and of Cunard crew and ships in World War One more generally. Queen Victoria will call at Cobh (formerly Queenstown) on 7 May, 2015, 100 years to the day since Lusitania was lost.

David Dingle, Chairman of Cunard parent company Carnival UK, acknowledges the significance of Cunard's history and heritage. "Cunard history reads like no other. For so long the heartbeats of Cunard and Britain have been as one and we intend to celebrate this landmark anniversary in grand style.

"These special voyages have been planned over many months to commemorate key dates in the company's history with all who wish to be part of Cunard's special and unique heritage. We look forward to delivering this year of spectacle and celebration to the many people who share the pride we feel in Cunard's ongoing success on both sides of the Atlantic and beyond."

"Given the backdrop and the historic bond with Liverpool, this gathering of the fleet will be the most magnificent of them all."

Commodore Christopher Rynd